MW01136341

Starting with "I"

PERSONAL ESSAYS BY TEENAGERS

Also by Youth Communication

THE HEART KNOWS SOMETHING DIFFERENT
Teenage Voices from the Foster Care System
Edited by Al Desetta
Foreword by Jonathan Kozol

OUT WITH IT
Gay and Straight Teens Write About Homosexuality
Edited by Philip Kay, Andrea Estepa, and Al Desetta

A TEACHER'S GUIDE TO STARTING WITH "I"
by Andrea Estepa

Starting with "I"

PERSONAL ESSAYS BY TEENAGERS

BY YOUTH COMMUNICATION

Edited by Andrea Estepa and Philip Kay

———

Foreword by Edwidge Danticat

Introduction by Andrea Estepa

PERSEA BOOKS

NEW YORK

The essays in this anthology first appeared in New Youth Connections, *a magazine written by and for New York City young people, sometimes in slightly altered form. A list of original publication dates is provided on page 182.*

For information, contact the publisher:

Persea Books, Inc.
853 Broadway
New York, New York 10003

Library of Congress Cataloging-in-Publication Data

Starting with "I" : personal essays by teenagers/by Youth
    Communication; edited by Andrea Estepa and Philip Kay.
        p.   cm.
    Summary: Essays by teenagers about diverse issues, from racism,
violence, and teen parenting to shopping for clothes and listening
to music.
    ISBN 0-89255-228-X (pbk.)
    1. Teenagers—United States—Juvenile literature. 2. Teenagers—
United States—Attitudes—Juvenile literature. 3. Adolescence—
United States—Juvenile literature. [1. Youths' writing.]
I. Estepa, Andrea. II. Kay, Philip. III. Youth Communication
(Organization)
HQ796.S8233   1997   96-48606
305.235—dc21   CIP
                                                               AC

Designed by Rita and Robert Lascaro
Manufactured in the United States of America
Second Printing

In loving memory of my grandmother, a born storyteller
Andrea Estepa

A Haydée, que me dio su mano franca
Philip Kay

To Peter, who taught me to listen to teenagers
Keith Hefner
Executive Director, Youth Communication

Contents

II. WHERE I'M FROM
Essays About Places

III. IT'S NOT BLACK AND WHITE
Essays About Race and Culture

IV. HE SAID, SHE SAID

Essays About Gender and Sexuality

V. BECOMING WHO I AM

Essays About Choices

VI. SPEAKOUT ON WRITING

Six young authors share their insights about the writing process

Foreword

IN THE FACE OF SILENCE
Edwidge Danticat

I remember walking through the doors of Clara Barton High School in Brooklyn for the first time, in September 1982. While negotiating new hallways and classrooms filled with thousands of students, I never felt more alone in my life. A recent immigrant from Haiti, I was still experiencing culture shock and bouts of depression over the other students' perceptions of Haitian immigrants, especially their tendency to call us Frenchies and boat people. At the same time, I was hoping to find new classmates with whom to build lasting friendships, and even from day one, I was already fretting over getting good grades and longing to discover the right extracurricular group that would allow me to indulge my one great love—writing.

Aside from my journal writing, I had no way to express these fears and anxieties—and the excitement one inevitably feels at starting a new phase of life. Being new at the school, I felt the school counselors were off limits, reserved for the truly troubled teens. My parents were hardworking and religious people. They had a strong sense of sacrificial duty; that is, they believed that anything worth having—like a high school education, for example—was worth suffering for. Besides, they were fighting their own battles in the larger world, struggling against poverty, racism, and xenophobia—others' fear of foreigners. My problems seemed small and petty compared to theirs. They couldn't just stop and take a breather from life. They always had to keep going, keep working, keep fighting to support our family here and other family members who were depending on them in Haiti. If not for writing, I would have been shut behind a wall of silence with all these things brewing inside me, with no one to trust, no one to tell.

A year after I started high school, I began to write for *New Youth Connections*, a channel of voices for New York City youth. My first piece was about exiled Haitian families, including my own, celebrating Christmas in the United States. It was extremely gratifying to see my words in print, to observe my classmates who knew nothing about me or my culture come to understand a very important aspect of my life through something I had written. From that moment on, I decided that I would become a writer, not only for the thrill of recognizing my name in a byline, but to break the silence that surrounded me, to bring to light some parts of the mystery that was my individual soul, to look at my life up close and invite others to do the same.

Later, when I was a freshman in college, as my final piece for *New Youth Connections*, I decided to write a more personal narrative about being a recent immigrant in New York. I wrote about my first weeks in school, how lost and lonely I felt, how overwhelming the whole experience had seemed. When I was done with the piece, I felt that my story was unfinished, so I wrote a short story, which later became a book, my first novel: *Breath, Eyes, Memory*. In her short poem, "The Three Oddest Words," the 1996 Nobel Laureate in Literature, Wislawa Szymborska, writes: "When I pronounce the word Silence,/I destroy it." Writing for *New Youth Connections* had given me a voice. My silence was destroyed completely, indefinitely.

In *Starting with "I,"* this collection of deeply personal essays—all originally published in *New Youth Connections*—the young writers, raconteurs, not only destroy silence but they also laugh at it, scream at it, and stomp all traces of its shadow from their lives. For they are not afraid to reveal their saddest, and funniest, most frustrating, and fulfilling moments while speaking from the very inner core of deeply personal experience. As I read these pages, I happily found myself peeking behind veils of silence, rejoicing at the candor and honesty, the beauty and the humor masterfully employed by young adults facing such life-changing issues as AIDS, racism, homosexuality, immigration, multicultural friction, sexual assault, child abuse, and other forms of domestic violence. At the same time I was just as delighted see these writers explore the nostalgia of childhood, recall their very first love, mourn the disappearance of cherished places, marvel at new kinds of music, and dream of the futures they'd like to have. No matter what their subject, all of these writers expose and revisit their emotions so clearly that it's very obvious that writing is for them, as it was for me, part of a long process of self-understanding and individual healing that has continued long after those essays were authored and published in the pages of *New Youth Connections*.

How I wish that I'd had a book like this as I entered the halls of Clara Barton High School that first day in September 1982. When I envision my four years there, I long to have these intimate and fascinating tales with me to cling to, like the private confidences of a good friend. I am happy, however, that this book is here for you now. For as I read and reread these essays, I felt as though I had been invited into the parlors and the kitchens, the hearts and souls of these writers. How blessed I felt to be in the company of such talented and courageous young women and men whose words will now be woven into the fabric of my life and whose voices I will take with me wherever I go.

I hope this book does the same for every one of you. I hope it makes you look at your own life in a whole different way. The truth is, we can all destroy our own silences by picking up a pen or pencil—by "starting with 'I'." That is what I did. That is what these young men and women did. By writing these essays and revealing themselves to us, they continue to destroy not only their own silence and mine, but also yours, too.

Introduction

By Andrea Estepa

getting a haircut. Going clothes shopping with your mother. Losing a favorite uncle to AIDS. Having a bottle thrown at you by a stranger on the street. Moving to a new neighborhood. Hearing the band Nirvana for the first time. Getting a job at McDonald's. Finding out that a friend has been shot. Moving into a dorm. Realizing that you're gay.

These are just a few of the experiences—some ordinary, some extraordinary—that inspired this book's young authors to sit down and write.

Many adults believe that the written word is dying, that kids today either can't or won't write. But in six years of working with teenagers, I've found just the opposite. Kids do all kinds of writing as part of their day-to-day lives: they compose raps and song lyrics, keep journals, write poems and love letters. They are inspired to put pen to paper by the need to create, to communicate, to figure things out.

It's true that many of these same kids struggle with or are bored by the kind of writing they're asked to do for school. The word "essay" conjures up the dry, the distant, and the trite. But when they are encouraged to explore subjects that really interest them, they find out that essay-writing can actually be fun.

The writers in this collection have discovered that essays can grow out of the same experiences and feelings that prompt letters and diary entries and poems. And that they can be written in the same kind of language—direct, colloquial, like a conversation with a friend. As Phillip Lopate writes in the introduction to his anthology *The Art of the Personal Essay*, "The hallmark of the personal essay is its intimacy. The writer seems to be speaking directly into your ear ...the personal essayist sets up a relationship with the reader, a dialogue—a friendship, if you will, based on identification, understanding, testiness, and companionship."

In this anthology, you'll find essays on serious issues like violence ("Revenge in the Hood"), racism ("A 'Nice' Neighborhood ...Where Nobody Knows My Name"), teen parenting ("Growing into Fatherhood") and AIDS ("Saying Goodbye to Uncle Nick"), as well as accounts of common teen experiences like getting a first job ("Climbing the Golden Arches") and starting college ("Dorm Life Is Heaven"). You'll encounter examples of humorous writing ("How to Survive Shopping with Mom"), travel writing ("Chinese in New York, American in Beijing") and autobiography ("I Hated Myself" and "Home Is Where the Hurt Is"). As you read, you'll feel as if you're really getting to know the authors because their stories are written like letters to a friend.

But there are important differences between an essay and a letter. However friendly or casual the tone, an essay must have a specific focus and purpose. It's not just a rambling account of what the writer did today but her reflections on a particular event or experience and why it's important. In an essay, the writer tries to underscore what's universal in her experience or to use the events of her own life to comment on a larger issue or problem.

A stranger's detailed account of getting a haircut, for example, would probably not be interesting for most people to read. But Anita Chikkatur's story "A Shortcut to Independence" is about much more than a visit to the hairstylist. It's about family relationships, cultural traditions, standards of beauty, and adolescent rebellion.

"For years," Anita writes, "I needed my Mom's help to twist my long, thick hair, which fell nearly halfway down my back, into a braid or even a ponytail. I hated that morning ritual because it made me feel helpless." But she was raised believing that being a woman means having long hair, and that this is especially true for "good Indian girls." Cutting her hair is Anita's way of telling her family (and herself) that she's not comfortable with the traditional Indian definition of appropriate feminine behavior and that she's going to figure out for herself what kind of woman she wants to be. Anyone who's ever fought with her parents over getting a tattoo or pierced ears, wearing pants that are too baggy or a skirt that is too short will be able to relate to Anita's story.

The other thing that makes an essay different from a letter is that the writing itself has to be entertaining, thought-provoking, or touching. Otherwise, no one is going to want to read it. You can't assume your audience will understand what you're talking about or be interested in your opinions the way you can when writing to a friend. You need to come up with vivid descriptions made up of concrete details, use interesting metaphors and emotionally charged language to draw the reader in and help her see what you see, feel what you feel.

For example, in an early draft of "My First Love: Too Much, Too Soon," the author recalled that when she first met her future boyfriend, she thought he was "ugly." I asked her to come up with a more detailed description of the boy, something that would enable readers to visualize him. She then added: "Roger's face was bumpy and you could see where he scratched his pimple and it burst. And the way he dressed! He had on rundown faded black jeans and sneakers with holes in them and a striped shirt with bleach stains on it." This gives us a much clearer picture of what Roger looked like and also tells us what "ugly" means to the author.

The impact a story has on a reader depends not only on elements like description but also on the writer's overall approach to her material. Delia Cleveland begins her story, "A Designer Addiction" this way: "My name is Dee and I am a recovering junkie. I was hooked on the strong stuff. Ralph Lauren wore my pockets thin. Calvin Klein was no friend of mine. And then Guess? what—I finally got the monkey off my back, although it took me a while to get on the right track." Delia goes on to describe her "habit," comparing the designers to "pushers," talking about how her mother begged her to "get help," and explaining how seeing other "users" destroy their lives is what got her to quit. She could have taken a more straightforward approach, but by weaving the addiction metaphor through the essay, Delia cleverly gets across how her love affair with name-brand clothing got out of control. It's also an effective way to get readers to see their own "habits" in a new light—is there anything that they're "hooked" on to an unhealthy degree?

Like Delia, Loretta Chan shows how a personal experience can inspire reflections that are more than just personal. In "Tired of Being a Target," Loretta describes how helpless she felt after a strange man threw a bottle at her. Afterward, she writes, "I wasn't the I-am-woman-hear-me-roar girl that a lot of people know me as. Instead I became one of those pitiful girls who can't stand up to a chauvinist pig."

But the incident does more than alter Loretta's image of herself; it also prompts her to grapple with the larger issue of women's place in society, of how their freedoms are circumscribed by fear. "We are constantly reminded that we are in danger," she writes. "People warn us that we shouldn't be taking the train at night alone, or at all, that we shouldn't be walking down a deserted street after dusk, that there are certain areas a young lady should never wander through. However, men can roam the entire earth with minimal caution." In the end, Loretta is left with a question: How can a woman live an independent life when she also needs to fear for her safety? "It's driving me crazy that I don't have a better solution to this problem," she writes. But the fact that she offers no easy answers makes her essay more satisfying to read, not less.

Many of the writers represented here use their essays to explore questions, doubts, confusion or ambivalence. The reader is invited to accompany them as they sort through their mixed feelings. The "I" who is telling the story often changes in significant ways between the beginning and the end. Take Allen Francis. A self-described "hardcore rap fanatic," Allen feels as if he is betraying an old friend when he realizes that he likes the music of the band Nirvana. Early in "A Rap Fan's Alternative," he writes, "Part of me felt that there wasn't room in my musical taste for headbanger vomit noise. How could I be devoted to rap and grunge at the same time?" Allen undergoes an identity crisis: Is he no longer the person he thought he was? What will his friends and family think? Gradually he realizes that it is indeed possible to like both: "My musical taste had room the size of a warehouse; I had just never bothered to fill it," he writes. By the end, Allen has reached a new, more complex understanding of who he is.

Others begin with a strong point of view, a clear message that they want to impart to their readers, and never waver. In "Yo, Hollywood! Where Are the Latinos At?" for example, Jessica Vicuña takes a stand on a controversial issue that's important to her. Disgusted with the way Latinos are depicted in many Hollywood films, Jessica argues that only Hispanic actors should be cast to play Hispanic characters. "I'm sorry," Jessica writes, "but I don't want to see Al Pacino play any more Hispanic roles like the leads in *Scarface* and *Carlito's Way*."

Jessica's essay demonstrates that you don't have to turn to an encyclopedia or newspaper to gather ammunition for an opinion piece. Her argument is based on her own observations through years of movie-going and TV watching. As a Puerto Rican, she finds many of the portrayals of Hispanic characters by white actors "unreal" and stereotypical. In her eyes, not hiring Hispanic actors for these roles is a form of discrimination. To help readers understand how she feels, Jessica asks them to imagine what it would be like if Hollywood were equally color-blind in its casting of other groups. "Think how silly the movie *The Last Emperor* would be if Jeremy Irons played the emperor," she writes. "What if Winona Ryder were one of the daughters in *The Joy Luck Club*? It wouldn't look realistic because they're not Asian, right? So why should movies about Latinos be held to a different standard?"

Although they address a wide range of topics and employ a variety of writing styles, these authors all have one thing in common— they are in the process of coming to terms with some aspect of their identity. They are exploring the factors that determine how they see themselves and how others see them. What's more important, they ask, the way we look or what we believe? What we have in common with the people around us or what sets us apart from them? Is identity something that we determine for ourselves? Or is it thrust upon us by family, friends, the larger society?

These questions are excellent starting points for personal writing, especially for teenagers. For many of the writers in this collection, negotiating the gulf between other people's expectations of them and what they know to be true of themselves is a daily struggle. Where others might see the black guy in the baggy pants and think "hoodlum" or see the Asian girl who always gets good grades and think "nerd," the writers themselves know better. As Jamal Greene, a black teenager who has been told that he doesn't act like a "real" black person, writes in "Color Me Different," "As long as other people expect me to act a certain way because of the way I look or to look a certain way because of the way I act, I will continue to be something of an outcast because I defy their prejudices." Writing this piece—which tells us how Jamal sees himself—is a further act of defiance.

The essays in this collection originally appeared in *New Youth Connections*, a magazine by and for New York City teenagers. (The author's age at the time of initial publication is noted at the beginning of each piece.) The vast majority of the writers were public high school students when they joined the staff; most are black, Latino, or Asian; some got school credit for their work and some were volunteers. They got involved with *NYC* because they enjoyed writing, because they were considering careers in journalism and wanted to experience working with an editor and getting published, or simply because they had something they desperately needed to say and no one they could say it to. Whatever their motivation, they all had stories to tell and a willingness to devote the time and energy necessary to tell those stories in writing.

None of the pieces in this book were just dashed off. In fact, they took weeks and months to develop. It's extremely rare for anyone— student or professional author—to produce a perfect first draft. In the initial rush to get their ideas down on paper, the writers in this collection left out many of the details, descriptions, and snatches of dialogue that you'll find in the versions published here. Working with an adult editor, they took their stories through as many as a dozen drafts. Questions were asked and answered, paragraphs were moved around, sentences were written, crossed out and sometimes put back again. Through this back-and-forth between writer and editor, the stories took shape: a focus emerged, unrelated ideas and superfluous information were cut, and the crucial events, characters and opinions were fleshed out. One of the best things about writing is that you can keep working on it until you get it right, until the words say what you want them to say. If you write something and you don't like the way it sounds or it doesn't convey exactly what you mean, you can erase it and start over.

Of course, revising can be difficult and frustrating. Sometimes it feels as if you'll never be able to get it right. These writers stuck with it because they knew that when they finally finished, a large audience of their peers was going to read what they'd written. That's a great motivator, but you don't have to be published to have an audience. We can write for friends and family members, teachers, and classmates. They can play the role of editor by asking questions and making suggestions. ("I'm not sure what you mean. Could you give an example? And I really like the fourth paragraph, maybe you should start with that.") Getting feedback from others can help a writer clarify what she thinks or figure out how to explain herself better.

Another way to improve your writing is by reading and that's where this book comes in. Some of the stories in this collection will remind readers of events in their own lives that are worth exploring on paper. Others may prompt a new understanding of the techniques writers use to make their work interesting or enjoyable to read. When a paragraph makes you laugh or cry or say to yourself, "Wow, I can see exactly what that must have been like," try to figure out what the author did to provoke that reaction. Then think about how you might apply what you've learned to your own work.

We hope this book will inspire teen readers to see new possibilities in the essay form and motivate them to use writing to reflect on their lives, argue their points of view, and entertain their friends. We also hope it will get teachers to see their students' day-to-day lives as worthy points of departure for essay writing. To help, we've included some reflections from the authors on why and how they write, as well as what they get out of working on these kinds of personal essays. You do learn a lot about writing, they say, but the real payoff is what you learn about yourself along the way.

A NOTE ON LANGUAGE

The authors of these essays were encouraged to write in the way that they speak. Their colloquial language and use of slang make their stories lively, engaging reading—especially for young people. It also means that this book contains some usages that are not strictly correct. As long as the writer's meaning is clear, perfect grammar is sometimes sacrificed in order to retain a natural voice.

While these writers have been discouraged from using language that may be hurtful or offensive to others, they were also urged to report the truth and to be faithful to the way real people speak. On the rare occasions where their writing includes slurs or profanity, we have tried to call attention to it with the use of dashes, as in "f--got" or "n--ger." The one exception is the story "The 'N' Word: It Just Slips Out" in which the author, a young black man, explores his feelings about using the word "nigger." Because the story is about the word's meaning and power, it seems inappropriate not to write it out. As you read, we encourage you to think about and to discuss what makes certain words hateful or offensive, why you think an author might choose to include an offensive or insulting word in an essay, and in what contexts, if any, it might be appropriate or necessary to use "bad" words in this kind of writing.

I.

Close to Home

ESSAYS ABOUT FAMILY

.

BROTHERLY LOVE

Jessica Vicuña, 18

*M*y mom was always working and my dad was…well, he simply wasn't around. Growing up, it seemed like my oldest brother Adolfo was the only one who made time for me.

Even when I was little, Adolfo always talked to me and took me places. We'd hang out in parks and watch movies together. He'd play stupid Ken and Barbie with me. When I was eight and he was twenty-one, he started taking me along to his college classes. I remember staring at him as he wrote down a bunch of squiggly lines and thinking to myself, "My brother is a genius." (I later learned that he was taking music theory and those squiggly lines were musical notes, not Egyptian hieroglyphics.)

But the coolest thing about my brother was simply the way he treated me—like I was an adult, even though I was only in the third grade.

My childhood Christmases were the best times because Adolfo made them memorable. He gave me cool dolls like She-ra (the female cartoon super hero and He-man's sister), Cat-ra (the female villain), and Thundercats while everyone else gave me corny gifts like A. G. Bear and Peeing Wanda.

When blizzards hit, Adolfo would carry me downstairs kicking and screaming because I knew he would throw me into the deepest snow mound on the block and leave me there. When I finally dug myself out of the snow, frostbite and all, I would try to run upstairs to regain my warmth. Before I could reach the door, someone would catch me in a bear lock. Yes, you guessed it—Adolfo. He would be hiding behind the door downstairs, waiting for a chance to throw me back into the snow. I think he liked torturing me, but I didn't mind. It was fun.

The fun lasted until I was thirteen. That's when all the child stuff was suddenly over and everything happened to me with a big bang. Like, dare I say, menstruation, low self-esteem, idiot boys, and just questions, questions, questions about life.

Instead of talking to Adolfo about the changes I was going through, I tried hard not to show them to him. I didn't want him to know; I was too embarrassed.

I was also afraid. You see, my brother is very old-fashioned. He believes that women should act a certain way and young ladies should behave in a proper manner. If I ever told him that I liked a boy in class, forget it, he'd flip out. And if I tried to disagree with him, it would be waste of time because he is always right.

I was afraid that if I told him the truth about what was going on with me, he would either preach or criticize or just make me feel stupid. It was easier for me to be the kind of sister who had a smile and good grades. I felt that my brother had me on this "good little sister" pedestal. I was scared that he would stop treating me like I was special when it was finally brought to his attention that I wasn't a cute little girl anymore, just a confused teenager. Part of me wanted to sit down with him and pour out my entire heart, but I couldn't do it.

Things got a little better when I started high school. Junior high had been hell because all the popular kids hated my guts. I had feared high school would be the same, but it wasn't. I wound up meeting a lot of cool, interesting friends, schoolwork was easy, and life was good—for the first few months, anyway.

It didn't last. By the third quarter of ninth grade, I was totally dissatisfied with myself. Schoolwork seemed to get harder and harder. Each test I took felt like it was written in another language because

I couldn't understand the questions. I was so discouraged I didn't even show up for half of my classes. Pretty soon, I was running an F average. I got angry with myself and felt even more stupid because I was flunking.

I was depressed beyond the definition of the word. I was failing school and didn't understand what was going on inside of me. How could I have let it get this far? I was out of control for reasons that I couldn't define.

I wanted to tell Adolfo—about the flunking, about the depression, about me and him, everything. But I didn't.

I hardly spoke to anyone in the house, and my moodiness was overbearing. My family knew something was up, but no one cared to find out what the problem was—except Adolfo. He noticed my change of attitude and confronted me about it several times. When he asked what was wrong, I would tell him, "Nothing," and change the subject.

By the beginning of tenth grade, my attitude was starting to bother him. So when I went away on a school trip for a weekend in mid-October, Adolfo decided to call up my school and find out what was up.

All through the trip, I felt nervous, but I didn't know why. I guess it was a liar's intuition or something. When I got home that Sunday afternoon, my brother was waiting for me, all disappointed. I knew it was about my grades. I just knew he knew.

"You know," Adolfo started saying, "I called up your school Friday morning."

"A-huhh?" I said, thinking, *Dead meat!*

"I was talking to someone who was your seminar teacher," he said in a nonchalant tone.

"Oh yeah, Leo, my teaching seminar teacher, and..." I was so freaking nervous.

"Fs? He said you've got all Fs!"

"I know, life sucks!" I immediately told him.

"Why didn't you tell me what was going on?" Adolfo asked calmly.

At this point I was ready to break the dam, let all that water that had been building up inside me break loose. I was just scared that all that water might start a flood, and I think Adolfo was scared too. I wasn't sure if he was ready for this.

"Well, Adolfo, it's like this..." It came out. The dam broke. I told him everything. About the depression and not being sure why I had it in the first place; about school and not knowing why I couldn't concentrate on my studies; and about every burning, nauseating feeling I had in the pit of my heart.

My brother Adolfo was sad. Every time I cry, it gets to him. His eyes get sad and his voice drops to a deeper range. In that moment, he saw the real me. The me nobody knew.

As Adolfo started to comfort me with words of encouragement and understanding, I started to see snippets of Kodak color memories. Like when he would pick me up and fly me around like a baby jet airplane. Or the time he put on this big scary hideous monster mask and chased my sister and me around the house like a madman.

I felt like I'd lost the little girl inside of me forever. And when my brother sat there and tried to console me like a therapist, I felt he knew I'd lost that little girl too. He sat there, across from me on the bed, just looking at me. No hugs, no kisses, just analytical talk.

This was the moment that I had been afraid of. But it wasn't what I had expected. There wasn't any criticism, no angry vertical vein line on his forehead, no preaching on how improper it was to keep things from him, nothing. He wasn't looking at me through the eyes of a big brother; he was looking at me through the eyes of an adult.

The funny thing about it was that I felt some form of respect from Adolfo. He was ready to move our relationship into a different realm. This conversation was the beginning of something really mature for us. I wasn't his little kid sister anymore, and we both knew it. And it was okay.

It's been more than two years since that moment, and a lot has changed. (For one, I'm not screwing up in school any longer. I changed schools and I actually like it now.) My relationship with my brother is stronger then ever because of that talk we had. I've gotten to know who he really is and to see him as a human being rather than the "giant holy brother" that I had made him out to be.

I don't feel stupid telling him about my feelings anymore. I can open up to him without being put on the spot. I'm not trying to be a good little sister anymore. When I make a mistake, I admit it and tell him. I decided that if he gets upset, then he gets upset, but so far he hasn't. He even took it pretty well when I started going out with this guy...until the lad broke my heart. Then my brother saw red. I guess the overprotective side of his feelings for me hasn't been put to rest completely.

My fear that my brother wouldn't like the grown-up me has gone and left without a trace. Now that I look back, I realize that everything would've been easier if I'd told him about my emotions sooner. Then maybe the whole flunking and depression fiasco wouldn't ever have happened.

But I'm actually glad that it did happen. Good things came out of what seemed like a period of hell. I've gotten to like myself more. I'm not afraid to make mistakes anymore as long as I learn from them. And I no longer run away from my mistakes; I confront them.

This change couldn't have happened without my brother's help. I want to thank you, Adolfo, for being there for me when no one else was. For being the best brother that any sister could ever have.

How to Survive
Shopping with Mom

Chris Kanarick, 17

*I*t's Saturday. You and your friends decide to go clothes shopping. Before leaving, you explain your dilemma to Mom, who is confused.

"You have five thousand dollars' worth of clothes sitting in your room," she says. (Mothers tend to exaggerate quite a bit.) "You mean to tell me that none of the stuff from last year fits you?"

There are a few possible answers to this question:

> a) It fits, but my little brother likes it. So being the kind-hearted person that I am...
>
> b) Mom, if I don't buy new clothes, those guys in the mall who work on commission won't make any money to support their families, and their children will die a slow, horrible death. Do you really want that on your conscience?
>
> c) No.

Needless to say, c is usually the most popular choice.

"Why don't I come with you?" she asks. Your first impulse is, "Oh, God, no!" But think for a minute. Mom's got the credit cards.

Call up your friends, tell them you can't go. "Mom got you, huh?" they'll reply sympathetically.

So you and Mom pile into the ol' family car and you're on your merry way to the mall. On the way there, Mom will tell you that she does not have much time to waste because she's got (INSERT NAME OF MEAT HERE) in the oven.

Next, she will tell you that she doesn't have much money, so she's not going to spend $10,000 (there's that exaggeration thing again) on clothes that you won't be able to wear again next year, anyway. She will explain what your brother/sister bought and how much it cost, just so you have an idea of what to look forward to.

As you and Mom begin your leisurely stroll through the first floor of the mall, Mom will suddenly veer off to the left, arms outstretched, eyes wide, and nose in the air looking like something out of *Night of the Living Dead*. Mothers can smell a sale from a mile away. There is no scientific explanation for this, it just happens. Follow her. You have no choice. Remember who's got the money.

Mom will stop and explain that your aunt's friend's cousin has a roommate who has a brother who thinks this store "is the greatest thing since sliced bread," whatever that means. Without waiting for a response, she enters and heads towards the rack marked 50% Off.

After finding fault with every item Mom picks out, explain that you went to her store, now she can go to yours. If nothing else, mothers are fair. Pick the most expensive store in the mall, and lead the way.

Once you get there, Mom will go off in her own direction, as usual. You'll pick out several items, which she disapproves of—all except for one shirt, which she complains about anyway.

"Twenty dollars for a shirt?" she'll say. "You'd think it was made out of gold!" She may tell you that she saw the same item in the other store for half-price. There's no way out of this one, so don't even try it.

After circling the mall several times, with several stops along the way, Mom will decide to head for one final store—a favorite among women, a last resort among men, the mother of all department stores…Macy's.

Mom will immediately head to the boys' department. One of the other major problems with mothers is that they forget that although they do give birth to babies, no one stays that way.

Set her straight. Explain that you belong in the men's department (although I think Macy's has a teen department for those of us who haven't got a clue what size we wear).

This will make her nostalgic, and she will tell you how big her baby is getting—you know the deal.

Mothers come equipped with a built-in tracking system. Somehow they always manage to find someone they know at Macy's. Mom will talk to her friend while you pick up several items. When you turn to show them to her, she is already behind you, holding up a shirt with little red and pink flowers on it.

"This is spiffy," she says. You recall a discussion you had recently about a flowered shirt in which your friend explained that if he wore it, "I'd be mocked, I'd be jeered at." "You'd be watered," you replied. The *Magnum, P.I.* reject goes back on the rack.

Trying on clothes can be a nightmare in itself. You put on a pair of jeans and they feel pretty comfortable—a little long, but that can be taken care of. So you go out to get Mom's opinion.

"How do they feel?" she asks. Tell her they feel fine. Next, she'll want you to walk around in them. So now you're walking barefoot around the Macy's teen department in a pair of jeans that you don't even own. Not too awkward, right?

She'll ask you to squat. Then she'll start getting personal. "How do they feel in the crotch?"

"Ma!" you exclaim. "Not so loud! They feel fine."

The next thing you know, she thrusts her fingers into your pants and is running them along your waist to make sure there isn't "enough room for three more people in there," as she puts it.

Now, some of you may be laughing at me and saying, "Oh, I don't know what you're talking about." But there are others—you know who you are. Just know you're not alone in this crazy, mixed-up world where mothers reign supreme. Someday you'll be able to stand tall like me and say: Hi, my name is Chris, and I've gone shopping with my mother.

A SHORTCUT TO INDEPENDENCE

Anita Chikkatur, 16

For years, I needed my mom's help to twist my long, thick hair, which fell nearly halfway down my back, into a braid or even a ponytail. I hated that morning ritual because it made me feel helpless. I hated the long hours it took to wash and dry my hair.

I wanted to feel free and independent...I wanted a haircut.

But I couldn't make myself do it. A haircut was a big decision. My hair was more than just a bunch of dead cells. It was a symbol of control.

I held back for about a year because I was afraid of what my parents would say. The last time I had it cut was when I was ten and first came to America. For my parents and relatives, long hair is considered an essential part of being a woman. Especially for "good Indian girls." Most of my female relatives have long hair, and change is not welcome. Recently, when an aunt got a bob, my mom said, "She doesn't look good at all."

Most of my friends didn't want me to go short, either. I'm not sure why. Maybe they were like me, afraid of change. Somewhere inside, I believed that the really beautiful women had long hair. I remembered someone saying that college guys liked women with long hair. (And college is the place where you meet your husband.)

But my friend Hee Won assured me that it didn't matter what people would say. She and I used to gawk at women with short hair everywhere, trying to decide what style would look best on me.

Finally, last May, I decided to do it.

I put it off for a month, until the last day of exams, because I didn't want too many friends seeing me with short hair before I had a chance to get used to it. Hee Won agreed to go with me because I would probably have chickened out if she didn't.

We walked around my neighborhood, trying to find a good but cheap salon. I almost hoped we wouldn't succeed. My stomach was queasy. (Do sixteen-year-olds get ulcers?) But we did, and the sign in the window said $10 For Cut, Any Length.

When we went inside, Hee Won and I looked through a magazine for a style. I found a model with a really cropped cut (like Julia Roberts's hair in *Hook*) and pointed her out to the haircutter.

I sat down in a chair and looked around, fidgeting. Hee Won sat down on a couch. I told her to come sit on the chair next to me. The stylist put a white sheet around me. I took a deep breath, trying to relax. He released my hair from the ponytail I had stuffed it into. He sprayed water on it. I babbled nervously to Hee Won. Then he started cutting.

The worst part was the crunchy sound when he first chopped off about six inches of my hair. I thought that maybe I should tell him not to go any further.

I could see my hair all around me on the floor. (And at any moment, my lunch might have joined it.) I guess my nervousness showed because the haircutter smiled and said, "You won't be needing that anymore." Easy for him to say. He and Hee Won were casually singing along to Gloria Estefan on the radio, while I was scared to death.

For the next part, he told me to take my glasses off. I'm half-blind so I couldn't even see my reflection clearly in the mirror, let alone what he was doing. But I took my glasses off anyway. By now, I had decided I should go all the way. Besides, how short could it be?

The next time I put my glasses back on, it was already over. Too late to change my mind.

I didn't know it would be this short. It was so short that some of my hair was sticking up. The stylist told me that was because my hair had to get used to being that short. Forget the hair, what about my parents? Panic time. Hee Won told me it looked great. I nodded distractedly and paid up my ten dollars. The whole affair had taken about twenty minutes.

I walked outside and immediately felt that everyone was staring at me. It's because you look great, I told myself. Yeah, right. It looked horrible, I wasn't meant to have short hair, it will never grow back, my parents will kill me...

"I'm going to the Village," Hee Won said.

I stopped second-guessing myself and decided to go along with her. But first we stopped at a store to buy a Knicks hat. It was partly to cover my new haircut (my paranoia hadn't gone away yet) and partly because I had always wanted one, but hats and my long hair wouldn't cooperate. Now the hat fit perfectly.

Cutting my hair was my way of rebelling against my parents. What I didn't realize was that doing it was only half the struggle. Now I had to go home and face them.

My dad was on the phone as I came into the living room. "What happened?" he said.

"I got a haircut," I said lightly, trying not to sound nervous. He was silent so I went to my room. I listened to the radio and paced. I stared at myself in the mirror, trying to get used to the new me.

When my mom walked in, I was reading a book. She stared for a moment. "I don't like it one bit," she said. "It screws up your whole face." I didn't know what to say, so I pretended to ignore her. I wasn't hoping for an "It looks great... I'm glad you did it," but I wasn't expecting anything that cruel. I told my friends that since she didn't like it, I probably looked great. I was lying, of course.

I consoled myself, thinking that at least my dad didn't say anything. Then I overheard him talking about my "awful haircut." Later that night, my mom told me that he yelled at her for "letting" me cut my hair.

My friends' reactions were more diverse, ranging from "I couldn't recognize you from the back!" to "You should be in *Vogue* modeling that haircut." A close friend, who is Indian and has hair almost down to her waist, wasn't too thrilled, but she said she was "getting used to it."

Another friend said, "You look butch." Huh? "You know," she explained, "in a lesbian relationship, it's the partner who plays the male role." Oh? I didn't know cutting your hair meant changing your sexual preference.

Five days after my haircut, I went to New Orleans to visit my relatives. Given my parents' reaction, I was very nervous about what they would say.

My aunt freaked. "I can't believe you cut your hair," she said, turning to my uncle. "She had such pretty hair." I still did. "I can't believe you cut your hair. You had such pretty hair..." Okay, I got your point already.

This was how my uncle introduced me to a guest at his house: "This is my nephew... uh... I mean, niece," he said. Ha-ha.

It got better. "She had long hair before," he explained. "I guess she hates to be beautiful." What was that supposed to mean? That I was ugly now?

I became convinced that the haircut was a huge mistake. I tried to tell myself that it didn't matter what my relatives thought. But I was really hurt by their insensitive comments.

We drove up to Atlanta to visit more family. The first thing Uncle Number Two said was, "You've changed." Fair enough. Then Uncle Number One (of New Orleans) said, "She fell asleep at the hair salon and this is what happened." That's not what happened, I protested, but they were too busy laughing.

Back in New York, I told anyone who would listen what my relatives had said. My friends consoled me by saying that they were just jerks.

It took me about two weeks to get used to the cut and a month to realize that short hair was right for me. As a kid, I had short hair because it was my mom's idea, and I let it grow out because she wanted me to. This time, I'll keep it short because I like it.

Needing my mom's help to style my hair made me feel young and vulnerable. Now I can style it myself (if you can call running a comb through it a couple of times "styling"). It is fun to run my hands through my hair and not worry about getting it tangled. It feels great to wash and dry my hair in less than fifteen minutes.

I'm also the kind of person who feels more comfortable in jeans and T-shirts than in dresses, so my new no-fuss hairstyle fits my lifestyle.

Since I've gotten my hair cut, I've learned a few things about beauty, too. I know that being beautiful has nothing to do with the length of my hair and that a short cut has nothing to do with being gay or straight.

Friends tell me I look older with short hair. Better yet, I feel older and more secure about myself. In spite of my parents' reservations and my relatives' stereotypes, I'm glad I cut my hair.

My Father: I Want to Be Everything He's Not

Troy Sean Welcome, 19

My father was very popular in Guyana, South America, where my family lived until I was nine years old. His friends used to tell me how it was difficult to walk down the street with him without being noticed. I could only wonder about that, because I never spent time with my father when he was around other people. I saw him only on those rare occasions when he slept at home.

My father was what you'd call a playboy. He had a son with one of his mistresses and a daughter with a second mistress.

But despite all of his faults, I still admired my father. When his friends heard me speak, laugh, or walk, they'd say, "That's Terry's son, all right." I was just like my dad, and I felt good about that. I was proud to be like him. He was everything I wanted to be. He was my role model.

In 1983, we came to America. My father and mother fought constantly. I hated it when they fought, because he'd hit her. He started disappearing for days and then weeks at a time. I'd only see my father on weekends. One weekend, he took my brother Rob and me to a Yankee game. I don't even like baseball; the only thing I liked about the game was that he was there.

But the time I remember the most was the weekend when he taught my brother and me how to ride bicycles at the track and field next to Yankee Stadium. I remember going down the straightaway part of the track with my pops at my side. I felt a bond with him.

Those weekends were great, but they didn't last for long. When I was eleven, I started to see my father less and less each month. I'd wake up on Saturday mornings hoping to see him that day, but most of the time I'd be disappointed.

After about a year he called and asked Rob and me to spend weekends with him at his home in New Jersey. Even though I was happy to be with him, I didn't show it that much. I was hurt because he had left us for so long. It was hard for me to show him that I missed him.

The weekend stays at his house went so well that he asked us to spend the summer with him. I enjoyed that summer. He'd leave money on my pillow before he left for work in the morning. I looked forward to hearing his van pull up when he came home. I felt mad good because I had a dad again.

It was the little things that counted with me. He could have beat me every day for all I cared, and I still would have appreciated it because it was my father who was doing the beating.

The year that followed was good because I saw him almost every weekend. Then one day my father picked my brother and me up and took us shopping in New Jersey. He bought us suits, shirts, and ties, and we went to his house in Newark, where he was living with a woman named Fay.

The house smelled like a bakery and there were a lot of suits lying on the couch. I had no idea what was going on, so I joined two of Fay's sons who were playing Nintendo with some guys from the neighborhood.

Suddenly my pops came into the living room, called me and my brother over into the corner, put his arms around us, and said, "We're going to a wedding on Saturday."

"Whose wedding?" I asked.

"Me and Fay's," he answered.

I had an idea that he'd say that. I was happy for him. I rejoined Fay's sons at the television, hoping to start a conversation because I really felt like I didn't belong. "Yo, you heard… your moms and my pops are getting married?" I said.

"We knew that for a year already, you just found out now?" Shawn asked.

I was embarrassed because my brother and I were the only people who hadn't known. I thought that everyone was laughing at me.

"Now he has new sons and he doesn't need me anymore," I thought.

On the morning of the wedding, my brother and I had to help decorate the hall where the ceremony and reception were to be held. It was hard work, but hours later the hall was transformed with tablecloths and all kinds of decorations. I didn't mind doing all that work because I was looking forward to being a part of the wedding.

But I didn't have anything to do with the ceremony. After it was over, I was still hoping to sit with my father, but I could have waited years for him to notice me.

I was disappointed and upset because I did all that work on the hall and didn't get to do anything in the wedding. I felt as though my pops used me as his maid, as though I wasn't important to him.

After the wedding I spoke to my father only when it was absolutely necessary. As years raced by, the number of times that I saw him decreased.

I was angry at my pops for treating me like a stepchild at the wedding, but I still needed him in my life. It was very hard, and still is, to be a teenager and my own father at the same time. I'd question whether I was good enough to be considered a man. I couldn't get through a day without stressing myself out about whether I acted, talked, or looked like a man. All that stress affected my life in more ways than one.

Finally, about a year and a half ago, after years of keeping my feelings inside and many, many sessions with my counselor, I raised the courage to call my father up and confront him.

"What kind of father are you?" I asked him. "You don't call, you don't come to see us. If anyone met me in the last two years, they'd think that I didn't have a father. I don't understand what's going on."

"Ah, um, I have been calling and coming by," he countered calmly. "But you are never there."

The way he spoke to me made me feel like we were two executives at a board meeting.

"You haven't been calling or coming 'cause I would've gotten a message," I said. "I think it's because you got your new sons and Karen [my older half sister] over there, so you don't need us anymore."

I was hoping that he'd say that it wasn't true and that he still loved me, but that didn't happen.

"I don't think you should be taking this tone with me," he said. He was starting to get upset. "You call me up and tell me this bull crap about—"

"Bull crap?" I interrupted. "This ain't bull crap. It's the way I feel. I'm telling you the way I feel and that's all it is to you—bull crap!"

"Okay, it's the way you feel. But I'm still your father and you shouldn't be speaking to me like this," he said.

"As far as I'm concerned, you're not my father. You haven't been and will never be my father," I told him.

"You will always be my son and we will be together in the future," he said in a patronizing voice.

"If you're not here for me now, what makes you think that I'm going to need you in the future?" I said. "Listen, I have another call so I gotta go, ah'ight."

Click.

The conversation pissed me off. First, he had an annoying tone throughout the conversation. It made me feel like he wasn't taking me seriously. Second, he made me realize that I was right—he didn't want me.

But I felt a little relieved to at least know how he felt. It was the hardest thing that I ever did. I was trembling while I was speaking to him. My emotions had grown so strong from keeping them in for so many years. It was good for me to get them out because now I don't think about him enough to get me depressed anymore.

Surprisingly, he did call me back a few weeks later. He told me that he wanted to hang out with my brother and me that Friday. I canceled my plans just so I could be with my dad.

At seven o'clock on Friday night I was waiting for him. Nine o'clock came and I was getting frustrated because I hate waiting for people. I finally decided to call and find out if something happened to him. Fay answered the phone and told me he was sleeping.

She woke him up and he gave me some story about having a long day. Then he asked if he could see me on Sunday and I agreed.

To make a long story short, he never came on Sunday. That's when I realized that I was never going to have him in my life again. I've neither seen nor heard from my sperm donor (that's what I call him sometimes) since that conversation—a year and a half ago.

My mother still tries to convince me that I should love him because he's my father. How can I love someone I don't know and who doesn't know me? I've managed to hide my feelings for my father so deep that I'd have to dig to find them. I still think he doesn't want me, but I don't care anymore. I realize that no matter what he did to me, it's no excuse for me to have a messed-up life. Strangely enough, he did teach me something.

He taught me that the best man I can be is his total opposite. I now know that having children left and right doesn't make a man. Staying around to raise them does.

I have vowed to my only father, God, that I won't raise my children the way Mr. Welcome raised (or failed to raise) me. I will make it my business to be a part of my future children's lives until I lie in my deathbed. They say that when you get older, you turn into your parents—I pray to God that doesn't happen to me.

SAYING GOODBYE TO UNCLE NICK

Josbeth Lebron, 17

*N*ick was my stepfather's brother. I met him when I was seven years old, and by the second time I saw him I was already calling him Uncle Nick.

It was just his way of being that I liked: he was honest, sweet, funny, and very understanding. He was the type of person who, the minute you met him, was immediately trying to make you laugh. He did everything he could to make you feel comfortable, and it worked.

I used to see him at least three times a month, usually at my grandmother's house. Every time I saw him I said, "Hi, Uncle Nick," and he always responded, "What's up, sweetheart, how you doing?" He always asked me how I was doing in school and if I had a boyfriend.

When it came to school, I never disappointed him since I always had good grades. When it came down to boys, I always responded, "No, I don't have a boyfriend," and he would say, "Good, you're too young for boys anyway." He always had new jokes and new ways to make me laugh. Uncle Nick was an all-around nice guy. I loved and cared about him very much.

Six years ago, I heard the news that Uncle Nick had the AIDS virus. He was twenty-seven, and I was twelve. My mother and stepfather sat my two stepbrothers and me down and explained the whole situation. I was shocked. I couldn't understand how a disease I had just heard of two years earlier could already be affecting my family.

Uncle Nick was such a cool guy; why was this happening to him?

My parents told me and my brothers that we shouldn't act or treat Nick differently, but I already knew that; I wasn't going to treat him like an outcast just because he was sick. But I did expect the fact that he was sick to show. The surprising thing was that the next time I saw him, he looked fine to me. I guess I expected him to instantly look like a monster, but he looked exactly the same as before.

I thought that maybe he wasn't sick after all. Maybe they had made a mistake—mixed up the blood samples at the laboratory or something like that. Or maybe his immune system was fighting it off, and he was going to be okay. I kept all of these thoughts in my mind so I wouldn't have to believe that Uncle Nick had AIDS. This worked for a while, but not for too long.

After about a year I began noticing changes in my uncle. They weren't drastic changes, but they were noticeable to the human eye. At first he gained some weight but he lost it quickly. Then his hair started thinning, which was obvious because he had always had a full head of hair.

About a year and a half after his illness started to show, his wife died. She had AIDS too. Before they got sick, they had been separated for a while and both of them got involved with other people. That was the origin of their tragedy, I think.

I didn't know Nick's wife that well, so her death did not affect me. I'm pretty sure it affected him because his son (who was also infected) had to go live with his grandmother. Nick had less hope because he was on his own, trying to fight the battle by himself.

About a month after his wife died, Nick stopped taking his medication. I guess his reasoning was, "What's the point of medication if I'm going to die anyway?" Uncle Nick had lost his hope for living. But his family still had hope and they convinced him to start taking it again. "What a relief," I thought, because to me, his not taking his medication would be like committing suicide.

It was around this time that the physical changes in Uncle Nick became drastic. He must have lost about thirty pounds all at once. It was very noticeable because he was about six foot one and was down to the bone. He looked skinnier than I do, and I weigh only ninety-three pounds.

He wasn't bald, but his hair was so thin you could see his scalp from a distance. He started getting lesions (they're sores) on his scalp and on his neck. He began losing his vision and having dizzy spells.

Since the changes were so drastic, they put a certain fear in our hearts—mine and my family's—that no one spoke of but everyone shared. The fear was that at any moment Uncle Nick could be gone. Seeing someone die of AIDS is like watching a person's life going on fast-forward. Their aging process hits full speed, and there is no way back. The hair goes. They walk and talk slower. Their face wrinkles and their vision blurs. By the time my uncle was thirty, he looked as old as fifty.

At night I cried and begged God to let Nick and his son be cured. Every time I listened to the news, I knew there was still hope. There was always new medication out there, and in my heart I always felt there was a chance that Uncle Nick would survive this and that one day we could all laugh about how scared we had been.

Since I first found out he had AIDS, I always kissed Uncle Nick on the cheek. I didn't think anything of it since I knew it wasn't possible to contract his disease in that manner. But when he started getting those lesions, I became scared for myself. I worried that I could catch some kind of infection from him, but I kissed him anyway.

One day Uncle Nick decided he wanted to treat my mother and me to some ice cream. By this time his hands were shaking and he had to walk very slowly. My mother figured he wasn't fit to drive, so she offered to drive his car. I remember him saying, "Nobody's gonna drive that car, only me, that's my car!"

We went and bought the ice cream and we all ordered different flavors. Uncle Nick wanted to taste my ice cream so he grabbed my spoon and took some. Then he joked: "Don't worry, it's not like I have a disease or anything."

I laughed but I was scared because I didn't know if he had any open sores in his mouth, and my gums bleed easily. Even though they say you can't get AIDS from things like that I couldn't help being frightened. So when he wasn't looking, I threw the spoon away and took my mother's.

To this day I still wonder why he did that. But I didn't say anything to him because I didn't want him to feel bad. I didn't want to remind him that he was sick. I wanted him to feel normal.

Uncle Nick fought for his life for as long as he could. I don't think he really believed the virus would kill him. He even seemed to be preparing himself for a new life in the future, as if he had all the time in the world. He bought a new car, rented a new apartment, and bought all new furniture and music equipment. He also got a whole new wardrobe. I felt bad about what he was doing (he was ignoring his illness), but he could afford to buy these things, and since they gave him hope, it was fine with me.

Last June, my mother and I received a phone call from the hospital at one in the morning. Uncle Nick was in the hospital and the doctor said he had only hours left to live and that we should go see him. My mother went, but I stayed home. I didn't want to see Nick in such pain. I stayed up that night writing poetry in memory of him. Fortunately the doctors were wrong, and my uncle continued to live but only for two more weeks.

While Uncle Nick was in the hospital, his mother used to sleep there to keep him company and to keep an eye on him at all times. Towards the end, while he was still fighting for his life, he used to squeeze his mother's hand because he didn't want her to let him go to sleep. I guess he knew he was on his way and he wasn't ready to go. He also didn't want to die in front of anyone. I knew he wanted to die in privacy, because every time my family went to see him in the hospital, he would always say, "Go home, do something, let me rest."

Once he said, "There's a door over there and I don't have the strength to open it, but if you help me I will go." In his dreams he had seen this door and it convinced him that it was time to take a rest. On July 13th, Uncle Nick said goodbye to his mother, who was going home for a few hours rest. As he was lying in the hospital room alone, Uncle Nick found the strength to "open the door." I hope that door led him to a new life where there is no pain.

His death didn't hit me hard at first because I couldn't believe he was gone. I saw my mother crying, but I couldn't cry. I said to myself, "Josbeth, what's wrong with you, is your heart made of stone? Your Uncle Nick is dead!" But I also thought, "The doctors were wrong before, maybe they're wrong again."

I didn't really believe Nick was dead until I went to the funeral parlor. I sat in the back of the room but I could still see him from there. Uncle Nick looked like he was sleeping, and I knew he wasn't feeling any pain. I stayed in the back and just cried as I watched my family pay their respects. I knew he would never awaken from that deep sleep. I didn't want to pay my respects because, like I said before, I wanted to remember him the way he was.

The wake lasted for three days. After the second day I felt guilty because I had never said goodbye to Uncle Nick. I realized this was the last time I would see him, and so I paid my respects. It was really hard for me to say goodbye, but at least I don't feel guilty anymore.

Before this tragedy struck my family, I had the feeling that we were invincible, that nothing could ever harm us. Now I tend to take life a little more seriously. I take into consideration the warnings that are given to me and I am very cautious about everything, especially sex (I abstain).

Now I don't think I'll ever forget how serious AIDS is, and I want other people to understand that too. You should never try to fool yourself by thinking, "That can't happen to me," because you're wrong. It could happen to you or to someone you care about. I lost someone very close to me, and the same thing could happen to you. And believe me, it's not easy to lose someone you love.

DAD'S HOME COOKING

Loretta Chan, 20

Tuesdays were quiet at Dad's restaurant. Mom would watch over those slow days at King Wah while Dad took me to Dr. Sanchez for my allergy shots.

On Tuesday afternoons, Lee, the nursery school bus driver, would take me to my special drop-off point on King Wah's block in Woodside, instead of leaving me in front of my family's apartment in Elmhurst.

Dad would greet me at the corner, carry me off the bus, and walk my cranky body to the restaurant's kitchen to wash off the miniature chocolate Hershey bar that had melted in my hand and all over the inside of my pocket. I always meant to eat the candy Mom placed in my jacket each morning for the ride home, but I inevitably fell asleep as soon as the bus started to move. At the end of my journey I awoke with my stumpy peapod fingers coated with milk chocolate.

While I waited for my dad to get ready to leave for Dr. Sanchez's office, Mom would seat me at the table reserved for peeling vegetables and put a huge box that reached my chin in front of me. It was chock-full of loose fortune cookies. Then she placed a stapler and a stack of crinkly-sounding bags on the table.

"Five cookies," she would remind me.

Once Tom, the Italian delivery boy, started a fight with me and said that my parents preferred to have three cookies in each bag. He accused me of being a wasteful brat for not being thrifty with fortune cookies.

When I went crying to my Mom's waist (where my face reached her body) she told the whole kitchen about it, including my father. Tom didn't hear the end of it for weeks. I can't remember if they were making fun of him for bullying a five-year-old or if he was really in trouble. He left King Wah shortly after that and went into the laundry business.

After my allergy shot, we'd head over to the Georgia Diner. I'd chow on melba toast and big, fat, smelly pickles while Dad ordered a hamburger for me and London broil for himself. Then for dessert I'd have strawberry shortcake and sip coffee with a spoon from his cup. And before we left, a big helping of dinner mints, which without fail cured any motion sickness I might experience in my dad's boatlike Coupe de Ville.

Between my graduation from nursery school and entrance into junior high, Dad never left King Wah. He never trusted anyone else to manage the restaurant (except for my mom, that is). I had a younger brother and sister by then. "Who is going to feed you?" my mom would reply when I asked her why Dad couldn't take Sundays off. My parents thought the restaurant would fall apart if he missed even one day. If that happened, where would the money to support our family come from?

Even on holidays, Dad had to go in for a couple of hours before the dinner rush. His day always started early and ended late. He was out of the house by 8 a.m. and never got back before 11 p.m. It wasn't unusual not to see him at home for days if our schedules didn't cross.

King Wah had grown increasingly popular over those years, and Dad had his regulars—the real estate brokers across Seventieth Street, the car mechanics and car dealers from western Northern Boulevard, cops, firefighters, teachers, dozens of families (mostly Jewish or Asian), and anyone else who wanted something more than the fast food that was so prevalent on the Northern Boulevard strip.

Wendy's, Burger King, Arby's, IHOP, and Dunkin' Donuts: their signs surrounded King Wah for a five block radius. Gargantuan and bright enough to light up a new moon sky, they flew several stories into the air above the fluorescent lobster sign my dad had hung proudly in the front window.

A person who stepped into King Wah would instantly be transported to China. On one wall, a panoramic picture of the famous Heavenly Palace (lit up by white lights hidden underneath it) impressively spanned an area at least five feet high and fifteen feet wide—from the entrance to the kitchen.

On the opposite wall, and about the same size, hung another illuminated panoramic photo—of the luscious green hills on the Yellow River. Dad had spent a fortune on these pictures and on his lobster sign. According to him, they were helping King Wah do great business.

During that time—my elementary school years—I had adopted English as my language and refused to speak to Mom in Cantonese, though I understood every word she said. My younger brother and sister couldn't even understand a telephone number spoken in Chinese.

Way back when we were still small enough for Mom to throw us into the car or threaten us with a wooden backscratcher, she tried to send us to Chinese school. When we got bigger, nobody could make us go. Nothing was more embarrassing than being stuck in a class with kids half our age. Our F.O.B. ("fresh off the boat") classmates were sent by their parents to preserve their culture. We were there to try to salvage ours. Ultimately, our stubbornness drove my mom to give up.

I began to see Dad on Tuesdays again when I entered the seventh grade. The restaurant was successful enough so that he could finally afford to take some time off. On those Tuesday nights, my dad planned to make dinner for me, my brother, and sister (who were now old enough to spend "quality time" with him) while Mom managed dinnertime at King Wah.

On the first Tuesday, Dad spent hours shopping for and preparing an elaborate Chinese meal of steamed sea bass, Chinese broccoli with garlic, chicken and bird's nest soup, and dried mushrooms in cellophane noodles. For dessert, lychees and grass jelly. These special dishes were not listed on the menu at King Wah because Dad thought Americans could never appreciate anything more Chinese than General Tso's Chicken.

Seconds after Dad had set his majestic piles of food on the dining table, my sister and brother made their selections and took their plates out into the living room to watch TV. Dad and I ate alone at the table he had set with chopsticks and ceramic soup spoons for four people.

On the second Tuesday, Dad surprised us with steak, baked potatoes, garlic bread, and corn. "Wow, just like at Georgia Diner!" my siblings exclaimed. American food was always Christina and Ben's favorite, as soon as they were old enough to walk to the Georgia Diner, where we went for dinner on holidays and some Sundays. Now in our own dining room at home, they played the roles of diners at a restaurant, sat at the table with knives in one hand, forks in the other, even paper napkins on their laps.

I was so mad at Christina and Ben that night. They made such a big fuss over steak and potatoes—a meal that takes no time to prepare. They seemed to have no idea of the trouble Dad had gone to the previous week. Even if they didn't like the food, they could have shown some appreciation for the effort he had put into it.

From then on, Dad would make steak and potatoes every Tuesday night. He sold out, making the meal that would get my brother and sister to pay attention to him instead of the meal that was special, that was his.

Tonight, I called my father.

"Are you eating?" I asked him.

"Yes," he replied and laughed.

I wanted to go to sleep in my father's bed tonight, like I used to when I was sick and my parents would sleep together in my mother's bed. They would tolerate each other's snoring for a night so that I could have a queen-size bed, a TV, and a bathroom a couple of feet away to soothe my discomfort. If I could, I'd get into his bed right now and bury my face in the sweet, faintly greasy smell of King Wah in his pillows.

HOME IS WHERE THE HURT IS

Zeena Bhattacharya, 16

For the first ten years of my life, I lived with my grandparents in Calcutta, India. I didn't know my parents at all. Then, one spring afternoon, I came home from school and found my grandmother packing. "Are we going somewhere?" I asked.

"Yes, to your parents, in Madras," she answered.

My parents had sent me to live with my grandparents when I was only a few days old. No one ever told me why. Nor did they tell me why we were going to see them now. Still, I had never been to Madras before, and I was very excited about going to a new place.

I went to my grandfather and sat on his lap. "Is it true we are going to Madras?" I asked. Just for a moment, I thought I saw tears in his eyes.

But he smiled and said, "Yes, I'm taking you there." Immediately I was reassured.

"Oh, boy! I'm going to Madras—to M-A-D-R-A-S," I shouted and ran out to tell my friends. Not once did it occur to me that my life with my grandparents was about to end.

At first, I found Madras very beautiful. It was like a big vacation for me and my grandfather with the two strange people I had only known from pictures. But after a month, my grandfather left. I was heartbroken—of all the people in the world, I loved and trusted him the most. How could he leave me with these people I had known for only a month? But I tried to make the best of it.

I tried to do everything my parents asked me to. They never really talked to me—just ordered me to do things or not to do things. Sometimes my mother would break into fits, shouting that I was such an obstacle in her life. My father too said I was a terrible burden. Soon their words turned into beatings.

My mother was very particular about how she kept her house. She would always remind me that if I weren't there, it wouldn't be such a mess. Once she started hitting me because she had asked me to make the bed in a particular way. But I had done it another way. "What difference does it make?" I asked.

That made her even angrier. As soon as my father came home, she told him that I was disobedient and had the nerve to talk back to her. He took off his belt and started hitting me with it. Then my mother grabbed me by the hair and started slapping me while my father continued with the belt.

Another time I had come into the drawing room not "properly" dressed for company. As soon as the guests left, my mother took a hot spatula from the stove and struck my cheek with it. My skin began to burn. I was so angry I said, "I hate it here, I want to go back."

When my father came in, he started striking me with his belt again. "Do you think we want you here?" he asked. "Nobody wants you here. Such an impossible child—but I am going to fix you no matter what. I am going to fix you—I swear." And he kept on hitting me.

At school, my teacher saw the burn mark on my face and asked me what had happened. After hesitating, I told her. "Your poor mother," she said. "Do you know how much it hurt her to have done this to you? But what else can we do? You children don't learn unless we hit you."

Another girl in the class raised her hand and said, "My mother beats me with a ruler, but it's only because she loves me." In India, it was only part of "proper discipline" to hit a child. Over there, it's the parents who never hit their children who are looked upon as neglectful.

Even in school we were beaten. Once, those of us who hadn't done our homework had to stand up and put out our palms so that the teacher could come around and strike us with her ruler. When she got to me, she gave me a reproachful look and said, "You see, you still haven't learned, you bad girl," and gave me my punishment.

At home, my parents said I was the worst kind of child ever and needed a lot of discipline. "A bad child," they would tell their friends. "So disobedient."

The fact that I was a "bad" child was the answer to everything. My grandparents had sent me back because I was a "bad" child. Everyone hated me because I was a bad child. I started to believe I deserved to be treated this way.

When I was twelve, my father was transferred to a job in the United States. As a teenager in New York City, it became even harder to deal with my parents. My friends would go to parties and movies and I would be stuck at home. Sometimes, when I did something they didn't like, my parents wouldn't even let me to go to school.

I wasn't allowed to go out of the house alone until I started going to high school. And even then I had to get home by 4:00 p.m. One time I went to McDonald's after school to celebrate the birthday of one of my closest friends. I stayed only for about ten minutes though, because I didn't want to get in trouble. I rushed home and got there by 4:20. My mother was waiting near the door and started slapping me as soon as I walked in.

When my father got home she told him to "ask her which guy was she f--king that she was an hour late." She said I had started to curse at her when she asked for an explanation. I was used to her exaggerating things and didn't even try to defend myself. I knew my father wouldn't wait to hear my side. And he didn't; he just started kicking me and swearing that he would fix me if it took his whole life. I just thought it was my fault. I shouldn't have gone with my friends in the first place.

My friends would invite me to go ice skating and to their parties. My parents would never let me go. After a while I just stopped trying to get permission, and the invitations stopped coming. I used to get depressed because I believed no one liked me. My grades started dropping.

Once I tried to join an after-school club. Since it was a writing club, I thought that I could just take the work home with me. But when I found out there were meetings I had to attend, I dropped out. I explained to my teacher that I had to get home by four o'clock and that my parents called every day to make sure I was there. "And what would happen if you weren't?" he asked.

"I would be in trouble," I answered, trying to say as little as possible.

The teacher wrote my parents a letter asking them to let me join the club, but they refused and my father slapped me. He was angry in a way I had never seen him before. How dare I complain to strangers about him?

Although I couldn't imagine telling an adult about what was happening to me, sometimes I would confide in my friends. "You should call the police," some said. But the thought of police coming to our house scared me. "Why don't you run away?" others suggested. Perhaps the worst thing I heard was, "Oh, you're exaggerating, it isn't so bad. Both of your parents are together. You are the only child. What are you complaining about? They're just overprotective."

Then one day, during another conversation with my teacher, I blurted out, "They hit me with a belt." At first I didn't think he was going to take me seriously. I thought he might say something like, "So what—I hit my kids with a belt, too."

Instead he looked at me very seriously for a moment and then asked, "When was the last time they did that?"

I remembered what my friends had said about calling the police. And I was afraid he was going to do just that. "It's really nothing—

I am the one who's bad, really," I said. I was remembering the grade school teacher who had labeled me a "bad child." I hated the way she had embarrassed me in front of the class, but I preferred that to having my parents reported to the police. I tried to explain to him that my parents believed hitting was the best way to discipline a child—that in India hitting a child was considered appropriate, even necessary.

"But with a belt?" my teacher asked. "I have two children; one is eighteen and the other is twenty-one. I have never hit them."

I just couldn't believe him. He must have forgotten. I didn't think it was possible to raise kids without ever hitting them.

"Well, you're not going to do anything, are you?" I asked nervously. Inside, I was thinking, "Oh, God, can't you just forget it?"

He explained to me that as a teacher he was required by law to report any child he suspected of being abused. The next day I was called to my guidance counselor's office. They told me that they wanted to call my parents.

That night I couldn't sleep. I just couldn't imagine how my parents would react if the school called. The counselor had asked me to describe how I thought my parents would react. All I could manage to say was, "They would be upset." But that was an understatement. I knew the end result would be that they would take me back to India. I wished I could take back what I had said.

I tried to figure out how to convince my teacher and counselor that talking to my parents would do more harm than good. Finally, they gave me a choice: they wouldn't call my parents if I agreed to go to counseling. Naturally, that's what I chose.

Once a week, I would go to my guidance counselor's office and she'd ask me what happened over the weekend, whether there had been any fights. Of course, it didn't change the situation, but talking about what was happening to me certainly helped me cope with it.

One time I told my counselor how my mother had asked me to iron clothes in a certain order and I had done them in a different order. Before, I had thought I was being disobedient when I didn't do exactly what my parents said. But my counselor made me feel that it was bad enough that I had to iron everyone's clothes. She said that my mother had no right to get upset over the order I did it in.

The counselor made me see that other kids did things that were much worse and yet their parents didn't treat them half as badly as mine treated me. Soon I began to understand that I wasn't responsible for everything and I didn't deserve to be treated that way.

Just talking to my counselor made me feel better. I wondered why I hadn't been able to get to know her before. I guess I had thought that all adults would be like my parents. It was a big relief to find out that it wasn't true.

When summer vacation came, I went back to India for a visit. One day I was walking through a park. Some families had built little homes there. One of the women who lived there was slapping a child so hard that I could hear it from down on the corner.

When I got closer I saw a skinny child, about four years old, being beaten by his mother. He was naked from head to heel and his skin was red. Tears were rolling down his face, but he wasn't shouting. It seemed to me that he was used to this.

Suddenly, on an impulse, I shouted, "Stop it!" The woman looked at me, astounded. "Do you want to kill him?" I asked more calmly.

When the mother finally recovered from the shock of my intrusion, she got very angry. "What's your problem, lady?" she managed to say. "He drank all the milk that we had for the week. Now his father is going to hit me."

She kept shouting angrily at me: "It's none of your business what I do with my children." Just for spite, she struck the kid again. "What are you going to do about it?" she asked.

A good question. What was I going to do about it? Call the Child Welfare Agency (CWA)? India didn't even have one, as far as I knew. Report the mother to the police? They would probably laugh at me.

Get her therapy? Take him home with me? When I didn't even have a home of my own?

I looked at the little boy's face again. The tears on his cheeks were almost dry. I turned away and started to leave. "Ha! These rich people think they can control everything," she called after me. "Hey, woman, if you love my son so much why don't you take him with you?"

Suddenly I hated myself. Why did I have to butt in if I couldn't do anything in the end? Did parents have eternal control over their children? Why was anyone else powerless to stop them? Why didn't they have a CWA in India? And even if they did, would it solve the problem? In the U.S., we still have cases of kids being killed by abusive parents. I realized I had to learn more about child abuse and what to do about it.

When I returned to New York, I decided that no matter what, I was going to help myself and others in my situation. I decided I wanted to do a Westinghouse research project on child abuse. In order to do that I would have to stay at school until 6:00 p.m. once a week. My parents still expected me home by 4:00 p.m. every day, but I applied to do the project anyway. I was determined that they weren't going to stop me.

My project proposal was accepted, but it was an ordeal to convince my parents to let me do it. But it was the new me that they were dealing with. I didn't wait for them to give me permission; I just started going. What could they do? Hit me? It seemed like they hit me no matter what I did.

Sometimes my father wouldn't let me in the house when I got home after 6:00 p.m. Once I had to stay out on the stairs all night. My mother said I was getting out of hand and my father agreed. "We are going to take her back to India as soon as she finishes this damn school," he said. This "American nonsense" was getting to me, they concluded.

One day I came back from school and my father started hitting me with his belt. I was shocked—usually he would at least give a reason before he started beating me.

I thought he had gone crazy. I just looked at him, too stunned to say anything. Then he stopped and said, "This is so that you can do your child abuse report better." Somehow, he had found out what my Westinghouse project was about.

Later my mother grabbed me by the hair and started slapping me. "A report on child abuse," she chuckled. "How daring!" She slapped me again. "How daring!" she repeated. *Slap!* "Child abuse, hah!" *Slap!*

Suddenly I couldn't take it anymore. I pushed her away. Before, I would just stand there like a statue and take it when she hit me. But not this time. I left the room and locked myself in the bathroom.

In the bathroom, I cried a little and thought about why they were so upset about my project. I knew other kids who were doing projects on dysfunctional families but their parents didn't get angry with them. It occurred to me for the first time that my parents knew that they were abusing me.

All along I had been thinking that they didn't know any better, that it was just the Indian custom to treat children this way. But they were perfectly aware of what they were doing. No wonder when my teachers spoke to my parents they always came away with the impression that my parents were just "overprotective." My parents had been treating me this way knowing it was wrong and making sure no one found out.

Suddenly I hated them. I had never felt as angry as I did that day. I used to think that it would be possible for us to have a reconciliation when I got older. But I no longer believe that there is any chance of that.

My parents still talk about taking me back to India to get all the "American nonsense" out of me. I have other plans, however. I'm going to stay here and study so I can help children like me as much as possible—not just in India, but all over the world. Because no one deserves to be treated the way I have been.

II.

Where I'm From

ESSAYS ABOUT PLACES

THE CREW FROM THE PARKING LOT

Ferentz Lafargue, 16

All the names in this story have been changed.

The parking lot behind Wertheimer's department store on Jamaica Avenue was once a place where a lot of boyhood dreams were born. Dreams of growing up and playing for the Yankees or Giants someday, dreams of meeting that girl, the one you knew was out there, the one who was made for you. My friends and I used to spend the whole afternoon there playing baseball, football, manhunt, and practically anything else you could think of.

One day we noticed a piece of wood in the corner of the lot. We found a rock to prop it up and made ourselves a bicycle ramp. We practiced jumping for a week or two until the wood broke and it was back to playing bike tag and waiting for the next thing to come along.

Every winter when it snowed, there would be huge piles of snow in the corners of the lot. We would start out by doing some light skiing to get warmed up and soften up the snow. (The skis were made of the finest cardboard we could find.) But we all know what happens when you put a bunch of guys somewhere with snow...SNOW FIGHT!!

The rules were simple: whichever mountain you were on was your territory and whoever was with you was your team. We would fight until one team captured the other team's mountain or the teams split up and we all started fighting amongst ourselves. When that happened it was every man for himself. We would go home looking like we had just climbed Mount Everest and sometimes I think that would have been easier.

We also shared a lot of disappointments in the parking lot. We felt bad for Ed when he didn't make the varsity basketball team. We felt sorry when Devon's girl Wendy moved away. (They were the royal couple of the parking lot.) When Abner and Carlos were sent to fight in the Persian Gulf War we all kept an eye on the news. There weren't any me's or I's in the parking lot—we were a team.

But these days the parking lot is just used for parking cars. We don't even keep in touch like we used to. Rarely will you see two of us together. Some have moved away; the rest just feel like they're miles away. At least to me they do. The only thing we all have in common is that we grew up.

When I look around now and see people that I used to be down with back in the days, I feel really sorry for some of those guys.

Devon was the superstar of the parking lot. He could throw, run, catch—the whole nine. We used to think he was the total package. We thought he would play high school baseball or football, then get drafted or get a scholarship, and go on to become a major leaguer. But instead of going out for one of the teams, he opted to be down with the fellas, hanging out and doing things like robbing people, stealing chains, or getting caught up in stupid gang battles.

Now he's one of the people who comes up to me and talks about how he messed up, how he should have stayed in school. The only things he strives for now are his own apartment, a G. E. D., a job, and a car. Devon's only eighteen and has been sent to jail two times already. The sad thing is he has no fear of going back.

Devon's younger brother John was a pretty good ballplayer too but more importantly he was a B+ student and a born leader. He was never afraid of being team captain. In fact, he thrived on it. He used to talk about joining the Marines and getting his M-14. Now John is seventeen and has a kid and he's not even close to a high school diploma. He was hardly ever in school last year. The word is that

John is dealing guns. An M-14 is probably child's play compared to some of the guns he's come in contact with.

Then there's Angel. Angel used to be my best friend and in a way he always will be. Angel had drive and determination. One summer he lost his glove and, since he was the only lefty in the parking lot, he had no one to lend him one. But Angel decided not to let that keep him on the sidelines. He found a right-handed glove and for about a year and a half he tried to be right-handed. He started doing almost everything right-handed.

Eventually he got another left-handed glove. But even after that you could occasionally see him tricking an opposing batter with a wicked right-handed curve ball. Angel hasn't dropped out yet, not officially, but I doubt he goes to school more than five full days a year. When he does go he usually cuts out early in the day. Now Angel's dealing drugs. He used to have determination, but these days the only thing he seems determined to do is mess up his life.

The sad thing is that these are the guys that little kids look up to. The other day one of my friends and I were walking down the street, and one of my little brother's friends came up to us with a fake blunt that he had rolled up, and he was telling us how good it was. This kid is ten years old at most. But you really can't blame him. That's what he sees around him. That's what's considered cool.

The ones who plan to go on to college go so that as soon as they're finished and have some money in the bank, they can move as far away from the neighborhood as fast as they can. My homeboy Abner, for example, hasn't even graduated from college yet and he's already beginning the process. He recently moved to a nicer neighborhood, and if it weren't for his parents you'd never see his face around the block at all.

He even started to forget people's names. There's one girl he's known for about ten or fifteen years now, and the other day he couldn't come up with her name. It made me wonder if he remembers mine.

Then there's me. I was the youngest kid in the parking lot, which meant I was last to get picked for the teams and the first to get picked on. I was like everyone's little brother. I never made it to the forefront; I just stood back and watched everyone else. I looked up to those guys. But I knew the real them. I was smart enough to learn from their mistakes.

They still keep an eye out for me. Every time one of them sees one of my articles in the student newspaper or hears about me doing anything else good, he's always ready to congratulate me and tell me to keep it up. It's almost like I'm their last hope of success: if I come out okay then they'll honestly be able to say they had a hand in raising me.

I intend to go to college and study communications and advertising. One day I hope I'll be writing for a big-time newspaper or working for an advertising company. Then I'd like to make sure my little brother gets his act together, help fix up my neighborhood, and do whatever I can to help out some of my old friends. But whatever I end up doing, one thing I won't do is let those guys down and mess up my life.

Writing this article I discovered I'm a pretty lucky guy after all. Remembering all those good times we had in the parking lot was enough to make me cry. I hope everyone has a parking lot in their lives. What good is a tree without roots?

AT HOME IN CONEY ISLAND

Sheila Maldonado, 17

I live across the street from the Atlantic. Not Atlantic Avenue, not the Atlantic Deli—the Atlantic Ocean. My house is just a short block away from the Coney Island boardwalk and the beach.

In many ways Coney Island is like other poorer neighborhoods in New York City. It's dotted with housing projects, bodegas, Chinese food places, and empty lots littered with broken glass. Most of the people who live there are black and Latino. It's the kind of neighborhood the media like to call "high crime" or "low income." What makes it different from any other "ghetto" are the beach, the boardwalk, and, of course, the rides.

But Coney Island used to be "the world's greatest playground." When I was little there were four separate amusement parks: Steeplechase Park, Dreamland, Luna Park, and Astroland. One by one, they closed down and the housing projects went up.

I remember hearing stories about the Parachute Jump, an old metal ride whose skeleton still towers over the beach near my building. They say some cables snapped at the very top and people went plunging to their deaths. That's why they closed it.

In those days, Steeplechase Park was filled with rides and games. I remember hiding behind my mother every time we passed this humongous swinging papier-mâché dragon that I could have sworn was eyeing me hungrily as we went by.

There was a game where you shot water from a gun into a

clown's mouth, making the balloon on top of his head blow up little by little until it popped, and another one where you tossed red plastic rings onto a bottleneck. If you won, you got a cheap stuffed animal. There was also a fun house, with mirrors that distorted your body and a laughing fat lady dummy in the window.

Most of those things are gone now. After they closed Steeplechase Park, my cousins and I used to sneak in and make our own amusement. We would get into the broken-down Tilt-a-Whirl. One of us would sit in a little mushroom-shaped car and the others would push, making the whole thing spin around. It was pretty dangerous, messing with that old machinery, but we didn't care.

Several years ago they tore out the Tilt-a-Whirl and everything else in Steeplechase Park and put in a running track and lots of grass where the stray dogs run. I walk my dog, Lola, on the beach and she plays with them.

Lola also used to play with the six or seven dogs that lived with the man in the old wooden house underneath the Thunderbolt, a broken-down roller coaster. It must have been something else to be constantly rattled by a roller coaster directly over your roof.

Last spring, there was a fire in that old house. The man wasn't hurt but his dogs died in the fire and all that was left of the place was a dark rectangular shell, a ghost, just like the structure above it. When I read about it in the *Daily News*, I cried. I used to pass by there all the time with Lola.

Astroland is still there, though, and still fun (if a little expensive). Some of the rides are better than the ones at Great Adventure, especially the swinging pirate ship. Of course, the best is the Cyclone, that rickety, elderly roller coaster that has been a part of Coney Island for more than sixty years. All the newer roller coasters are made of metal and have real smooth rides, but the Cyclone is made of old wood and you feel every bump.

Every summer four million people still come to ride the Cyclone and Deno's Wonder Wheel and to go to the beach. Hordes of them come rushing out of the Stillwell Avenue subway station and invade the neighborhood. They come in waves—wearing swimsuits, tank tops, and sandals, with a cooler in one hand and a radio in the other. The cars swarm down Surf Avenue near the boardwalk, fighting each other over a handful of parking spaces.

When they leave, they leave a mess. On the wooden planks of the boardwalk they leave chewed-up ears of corn, greasy wooden shish-kebob sticks, half eaten candy apples, and paper plates with leftover shrimp and french fries. The sidewalk outside Nathan's (the original hot dog stand) is littered with napkins smeared with ketchup, mustard, and relish. And the wood of the boardwalk next to the kiddie park is stained with all the oil and grease.

The beaches are in similar condition—at least the most popular spots, the ones right across from the rides and the aquarium and closer to Brighton. There, the beach is as flat as the boardwalk. The sand is covered with tiny broken seashells and packed down by the masses of people.

Farther down, near where I live, the beach is cleaner. The sand is soft and fluffy. Most people don't dare venture that deep inside Coney Island. If you want to get an idea of what they're afraid of, take a walk along the beach. You'll see the usual crack vials, and many a used condom left over from those hot, romantic summer nights. I've also found candles on the big rocks by the water, and feathers peeking out of the sand, still attached to dead chickens. Some of the people in the neighborhood practice Santería, a Caribbean religion that mixes African religion with Catholicism—a little like voodoo.

A few homeless people find shelter under the boardwalk; they hang up sheets and lay out their old clothes, empty cans, and plastic bags full of things they've collected on the streets. Even though the boardwalk doesn't provide them with walls, it does give them a roof over their heads. In the winter, they make fires on the beach and keep warm in tents. Some of them even have dogs, strays that probably approached them for food when they barely had any themselves.

At night, drug dealers hang out on the boardwalk and down below. The boardwalk is kind of scary at night. It's big and quiet and lonely and you never know who or what is going to pop out at you. It's not as romantic as you might think.

Every few years we hear some recycled, disguised-as-new rumor about a developer who's going to build us a stadium where Steeplechase Park used to be—a real New York home for our football teams that went to play in New Jersey. Or we hear that someone wants to rebuild the old rides completely and make Coney Island everything it once was and more. It gets a few minutes on the six o'clock news and we dream a little. But after a few months, we stop waiting for the construction trucks to roll in.

The Parachute Jump is being saved as a landmark. We've gotten a few new houses and soon there'll be some more stores, but mostly things in Coney Island get torn down instead of built up. In the good old days, people thought it would always be "the world's greatest playground." They could never have imagined it the way it is now.

Still, I've always thought if you have to live in a "bad" neighborhood, live in Coney Island. Sitting on the boardwalk or walking on the beach, you can see the entire sky. There are no buildings to block the view, no car exhaust or smoke to fog up the sky, just the sun, wrapped in a patchwork of bright colors and pastels, nodding off into the sea. At least they can't tear down our sunsets.

ANTIGUA: ALMOST PARADISE

Jillian Braithwaite, 18

"*G*ad e cold!" was my first thought after going through Customs and walking outside. People were walking around the airport in shorts and tank tops and there I was, shivering in my borrowed coat.

Making the transition from the weather in Antigua to the weather in New York was one experience I could have done without. Even though it was August, I was freezing.

I had been to New York a couple of times before, and it wasn't very dear to my heart. On one visit, my cousin and I were returning from the park one day, and as we were going into the elevator, a man got on with us. When the doors opened on the fifth floor, he snatched my chain. He was never caught. New York still owes me a fourteen-karat-gold necklace.

New York is a great city, but it's nowhere near as beautiful as Antigua, a small island in the Caribbean. My whole country could fit in the borough of Queens and there would still be room left over. But it has room for 365 beaches, one for every day of the year. (When it's a leap year, you take a shower on the extra day and repeat the process all over.)

The water in Antigua is a beautiful deep blue-green, and the sands are white and gold. When you walk you feel the warmth right through your soul. At New York beaches the water is so murky you can't even see your feet and the sand is just a few shades lighter.

I grew up in St. John's, the capital. Every Saturday morning I used to wake up early to go to market. When I arrived, I saw people coming off buses from all over the island to buy fruits, vegetables, meat, and fish.

The market is like a huge kaleidoscope—reds of apples and beets; greens of okra, cabbage, fresh figs, and papaya; oranges of carrots, sweet potatoes, and pumpkins; and yellows of grapefruits, pineapples, and bananas.

The meat and fish market is in a separate building. Here you see butchers in their stalls chopping up whole cows, their once-white smocks all bloodstained. Sometimes you have to hold your nose. Other vendors sit with big baskets filled with doctorfish, angelfish, snappers, barracuda, shark, crab, shellfish, and all types of seafood.

In Antigua we use what Mother Nature provides as best we can and try not to waste anything. I used to have mango, coconut, lime, tangerine, orange, passion fruit, soursop, and pear trees right in my backyard.

I miss being able to go out back and pick a fruit, wash it, and then eat it. In New York I can only dream of doing things like that. The people in my building use the little yard at the back as a convenient garbage dump.

But in some ways, life in New York is easier. Students here are always complaining about how unfair the school system is, that they can't do anything they want. But in comparison to the school system in Antigua, you people are living in the lap of luxury.

Here I'll sit in class and watch students insult their teachers and think to myself, "They wouldn't last a day in Antigua. They'd have more welts on their backs than a tiger has stripes."

Teachers there don't take any lip from students. In my old school if you had so much as the top button of your uniform (that's right— uniform) open, you received one demerit. Three demerits equaled one detention and every Thursday at three p.m. that's where you'd find me.

In the primary school that I attended, two bells were rung after recess. At the sound of the first you were supposed to freeze, stop whatever you were doing.

When the second bell rang you went back to class. No side trips to the bathroom, and—as I found out the hard way—no side trips to buy candy. The first and last time I tried doing that, the headmaster caught me and I got three lashes across my back with his infamous belt.

It's rare that you get beaten in secondary school, but it does happen sometimes. My brother's headmaster would make students kneel on gravel and then beat them with a tamarind switch.

One reason I like New York is because if a teacher tried to do something like that, it would be the last time she raised her hand to anyone.

Parents in the United States are not as strict with their children as Antiguan parents either. American parents encourage their daughters' interest in boys. They allow them to wear makeup at thirteen or fourteen and let them bring their boyfriends home to meet the family.

If you're an Antiguan girl, you don't talk to your parents about makeup before sixteen or in some cases eighteen, and you don't talk to them about boys ever.

For the last four years I've been living in the Bronx and I must admit, I do enjoy being able to do certain things that I wouldn't have dared to do in Antigua—like walking out of school anytime I want to without having to ask permission. But then I remember the things I miss most about Antigua—like all the open space. In New York all you see are big, ugly buildings and some garbage here and there to brighten the place up.

If Antigua had all the opportunities that New York has, I would be back there so fast that Superman would be the one asking if I was a bird or a plane.

CHINESE IN NEW YORK, AMERICAN IN BEIJING

Kim Hoang, 17

When I was growing up and people asked me what I was, I would immediately say that I was Chinese even though I was born and raised in New York City. I always acknowledged my Chinese roots, but sometimes I felt stupid for not knowing more about my ancestry and about a culture that has, in fact, influenced the way I live and think.

I am American, but there are things about my life that are distinctly Chinese. I eat Chinese food every night with chopsticks. I can understand Cantonese Chinese although I cannot really speak it. I go to family weddings in which the bride usually wears a white wedding gown in the morning and a cheong sam, a traditional Chinese silk dress, at the evening banquet. I celebrate the annual Chinese New Year festival with friends and family, and watch the sidewalk dragon dances in Chinatown.

These things are part of my life that came from China, a place I knew very little about. I wanted to go there and see it for myself. I hoped a trip to China would bring me closer to my Chinese side. When I mentioned my interest in traveling to China, my mom agreed immediately. She's never forced me to learn Chinese traditions, but I knew she would be pleased that I was ready to learn more about where my ancestors came from. Besides, my older sister was already there studying and I could stay with her and our relatives.

As I left for China last summer, I hardly felt the emotions I thought I would. I didn't cry when I said goodbye to my mother. I didn't cry when the plane took off, and I didn't even cry when I began to feel ill on the plane because of all the junky airline food.

But I did cry when we landed. I remember having this great feeling of awe and excitement, and I couldn't contain it. I envisioned all the new things I was going to see and all the relatives I would finally meet. Landing was so final. There was no going back, and all I could do was soak up every ounce of culture I possibly could.

My sister picked me up at the airport in China's capital, Beijing, and we boarded a minivan, China's cheaper version of a regular taxi. When we arrived at our relatives' apartment complex, I saw an eighty-year-old man and woman I vaguely remembered from photographs. They were my aunt and uncle on my father's side. It turned out that the last time they had seen me was when I was three and they were in America for a visit.

They went on and on about how I looked so much like my father. They said this all in Chinese and I could understand every word of it. But I couldn't express my feelings. All I could do was nod and smile, and they laughed, knowing that I couldn't talk to them.

It was apparent from the first day I spent in Beijing that I had virtually no chance of sneaking into the crowd and living like a native. The fact that I couldn't understand Mandarin Chinese blew my cover. (Although China has one written language, it has dozens of spoken languages. My mother taught us Cantonese, which sounds nothing like Mandarin.)

Everyone in Beijing spoke so fast and my sister, who was studying Mandarin, had to translate everything for me. Not being able to speak the language meant I had no freedom. I couldn't buy my own clothes or order my own meal. I couldn't even buy my own water. I felt like a three-year-old who had to ask her mother for everything.

The funny thing is that when I'm in America, Chinese people on the street ask me for directions in Chinese and expect me to answer them flawlessly in the same dialect. I feel bad when I can't answer them.

In China, however, people saw me and assumed that since I wore blue jeans and Nikes and carried myself differently (staring at every building with amazement and looking at every passing bicycle and every person with genuine interest, like most tourists do), I couldn't possibly understand a word of Chinese or anything about China.

People were surprised that I could understand the simplest Mandarin phrases (like "It's time for dinner" and "Did you have fun today?") without their having to translate for me. It's like I was living in two worlds and even though I was a part of both, I didn't fit into either of them perfectly. In America, I am Chinese but when I was in China, I was American.

What made matters worse was that my sister sometimes encouraged me to be silent so that we would get better rates for things. When we bought tickets to get into the Forbidden City (the ancient home of the emperors), for example, my sister told me not to say a word. She said that many museums and parks charge a higher admission price (sometimes three times higher than for a native) if they know you're a tourist. I never found out if this was legal, but it was widely done.

Keeping silent made me feel all the more foreign. It was a constant reminder that I could never fully assimilate into life there. I stuck out, and I began to feel extremely paranoid walking down the street. I felt like I had this big sign on my back that said, Kick Me, I'm an American.

Other times, though, I felt so connected to China. One night I looked out the window next to my bed. I saw the black sky and the bright stars and I felt like I was home. Other times I felt like I had been there before. I saw busy street markets with people haggling for the lowest prices. Traffic was horrible, and of course, almost every face you saw was Chinese. I had seen all of this in Chinatowns in New York, Boston, and Toronto. I was surprised at the similarities, but there were differences too: in America, I can always walk a few blocks or take the subway and once again mix with people of different races and cultures.

I visited many places while I was in China, but it was Tiananmen Square that had the biggest impact on me. This was where people gathered to listen to Mao Zedong's speeches as he spoke on a rostrum high above the square. (He was the founder of Communist China.) It was also the site of the 1989 Tiananmen Square Massacre, in which thousands of students demonstrating for democracy were killed after government troops opened fire.

The square is an open space where both tourists and natives hang out. Walking across the stone tiles, I remembered the news footage of Tiananmen Square, filled with tanks and chaos. I realized I was standing where many people had died for their cause, people who weren't that much older than I was.

One of the final things I did during my trip was talk to my uncle. Although I had been eager to chat with him, there never seemed to be enough time. (I was always sightseeing and he worked at a chemical company during the day.) I knew my uncle spoke fluent English, so talking wouldn't be a problem. (He had graduated from college in the United States before returning to his family in China.)

We talked for more than two hours, mostly about Tiananmen Square. My uncle said he thought that the students could have used a less dangerous method to obtain their goal and that they could have tried harder to work with the government. Although he still supports Communism, he thinks that all governments have their flaws and that there will be more demonstrations for freedom in China.

I wish I could've talked with my uncle longer. He has seen so many things in his lifetime—the end of the emperors, the birth of Communism—and I didn't have time to hear all that he had to say. But I was glad for what I did learn. Hearing his first-hand accounts made the recent events of Chinese history seem real to me. They weren't just facts in a book or images on a television screen anymore.

It's been a year since my trip to China, and the things I remember most are not the big places but the small things. The hot buses that my sister and I took to Tiananmen Square. The imitation Good Humor ice cream we bought to cool down since many of the museums didn't have air conditioning.

I still want to know more about China and Chinese culture. It may be a while before I have a chance to go back, but in the meantime I'm taking Mandarin classes and I'm volunteering at New York's Chinatown History Museum to learn more about the Chinese in America.

I had wanted China to bring me closer to the Chinese culture and heritage I knew so little about. But the trip brought into perspective the two sides of my life. I can enjoy the freedoms I have in America, like the freedom of speech. And I can also relate to the history of China and its customs. I now realize that who I am is a combination of the two.

A "Nice" Neighborhood...
Where Nobody Knows My Name

Sung Park, 15

Whoosh, whoosh! My neighbors are playing basketball again...at one o'clock in the morning. It's just my luck that I get stuck next door to these people who think that playing sports at all hours of the day is normal.

My neighbors are the Arnolds. That is not their real last name. I don't know their real name, so I nicknamed them the Arnolds. They live right next door to me in Forest Hills, Queens, and have lived there for the last seven years. Aside from their odd basketball-playing hours, I don't know much about them.

No one knows each other here. Correction—my family does not know anyone here. Maybe it's because we don't fit in. After all, we must be the only Asian people within a one mile radius.

Everyone is basically white and Jewish, but my family doesn't mind. We're content with just living here, particularly my dad. He was proud that we were able to move to a "white" neighborhood, that we would no longer have to be grouped with all the other Asians who live in clusters in Woodside or Flushing—where we used to live.

When we moved to Forest Hills, we did everything we could to get to know our neighbors. We tried to be friendly and hoped that our family would fit in. I remember my father inviting the people across the street to our house for Easter dinner. And for Labor Day. And Thanksgiving...they never accepted. They never even gave us an explanation. "Something to do," was mumbled into our ears as they continued washing their white BMWs. (The only kinds of cars people own in my area are BMWs or Mercedes. We have an old blue Volvo.)

The rest of the people living around us would invite themselves over to each other's houses almost every week and even go on vacations with each other. My family wasn't asking to spend a week at a resort with them, but knowing their names would have been nice.

I guess my family didn't know when to quit, especially my dad. No matter how rude our neighbors were, he kept on talking to them, waving and yelling, "Good morning!" to the people across the street. They'd just keep watering their lawns, eyes downcast.

I remember one summer a few years back, when my family had planted some tomatoes in our backyard. The plants exploded with them at the end of the summer and we had more than we knew what to do with.

My parents filled a basket with them, and I mean it was big—they had a hard time carrying it out the door. They casually sauntered over to the Arnolds and offered them some of our "harvest." The Arnolds just gave them a look that said, "We wouldn't touch that stuff with a ten-foot pole."

My dad looked sort of depressed and upset. He was really offering an olive branch to our neighbors, and they were nothing but ungrateful, prejudiced people. I started to get really, really steamed. I mean, who did they think they were to treat us like we were common criminals or worse? Just because our eyes slant down and our skin is a shade more yellow than theirs?

You may be wondering if our neighbors' behavior was so chilly because we offended them somehow. I doubt that we would be able to offend the entire neighborhood by offering food to them. Or you may be wondering if that's all they did to us—ignore us. Big deal, it's not a crime. It's not as though they were beating us to death or throwing garbage at us. But believe me, when you see everyone around you being friendly with each other and barely giving you a nod of acknowledgement, it is hard not to be bitter about it.

Still, in spite of the way our neighbors have treated us, I can't stand the idea of leaving Forest Hills. I've gotten so used to the environment. It's very pretty here. Small, quaint houses are lined with either white picket fences or sturdy black metal ones. In the southern part of the neighborhood, the houses are at least one hundred years old, although some are newly renovated. The old is blended in with the new, and all the houses are tasteful, not tacky-looking.

The streets are not paved but have cobblestones. There is a bridge that connects one apartment building to another and all the architecture is very old-fashioned. It's got greenery and big bushes dotted with small rosettes in the spring, and there are little pots of Swedish ivy on every corner. In the winter, the terrain is perfect for sledding. It reminds me of the New England scenery I see on postcards.

The neighborhood is also very safe compared to other places I could be living in—no burglaries or drug addicts hanging out on street corners. I don't have to worry about getting mugged every day, like I would in many of the neighborhoods where Asian immigrants live. Flushing, for example, is full of gangs that bother people on a daily basis.

Even if it wasn't dangerous, I don't think that I would be happy living in an all-Asian neighborhood. I don't speak Korean, so I wouldn't be able to mix with a lot of the people in an area filled with recent immigrants. And I don't really want to be grouped with all the other Asians who struggle and are considered a minority. I never considered myself as anything but a normal person. I never even gave one thought to my race until I started living in Forest Hills. I never encountered racism before.

But because I like other things about the neighborhood so much, I try to ignore the hostility around me and just keep to myself. I hope I'm not encouraging racism by not expressing my feelings to my neighbors, but I don't know any other way to deal with people concerning discrimination. It is not as though they would admit what they are doing if I spoke to them about it.

I feel like I'm saying that it's okay to ignore people who are different from you and that it's also okay not to care about your own race, and I feel guilty about that. But I don't know what to do about it.

When I become an adult and get a place of my own, I hope that there is not much racism, but as long as it doesn't get violent or vindictive, I'll let sleeping dogs lie. A diverse place where everyone can just accept each other would be heaven for me. But since I can't live in that kind of fantasy world, I have my priorities straight and safety is at the top.

I don't want to live in fear and wonder if I'm going to die if I leave my house. I'd like to live in a place that's pretty and safe like Forest Hills—minus the racism. I hope I won't have to experience what I'm going through now in the future. But I could live with it— I have lived with it for the past seven years.

Still, I can't help getting a chill down my spine sometimes as I'm passing by other homes on my block. The houses are so unwelcoming that I can't help feeling bitter hostility surrounding me. I'm reminded of it every day. I saw a row of tidy bright yellow tulips in a neighbor's front yard on a clear blue afternoon, growing quite nicely. I wondered, "How can a person grow delicate flowers with such loving care and give my family the cold shoulder all the time?"

It's sad to think people won't let you into their lives just because of some superficial reason. I hope to change that illogical reasoning someday when I'm older and more experienced to handle segregation, although I doubt I could be more experienced than I am now. I feel like I've aged fifty years instead of seven since I've moved to Forest Hills.

REVENGE IN THE HOOD:
A DEADLY GAME
Michelle Rodney, 17

I was watching the *Richard Bey Show* when the phone rang. It was my girlfriend Nicole.

"Hey," she asked, "what you doing?"

"Nothing."

"Michelle, you won't believe what happened. Kenyatta got shot right across the street from my house."

"What?" I couldn't believe it. "I'm coming over soon," I told her, and hung up the phone.

Kenyatta was a twenty-two-year-old resident of East Flatbush, Brooklyn. He was just a regular neighborhood guy I saw almost every day, a sweet-talking cutie who stood on the corner for a living. I guess I thought he would always be there. I guess we both did.

I left my house around twelve o'clock that afternoon to make the six block journey to Nicole's house. Halfway there I saw a guy I know named John. He was talking to another guy named Steven who, I guess, was breaking the bad news to him. Before I could get over to talk to them, John got really mad and started to yell, "How the f--k could that happen?" I decided to walk on.

A block later, I saw Billy, another friend of mine. He came over and kissed and hugged me and asked if I had heard the news.

"Yeah, that's really sad," I said.

"Hurry up and leave the neighborhood and go to college, all right, Michelle?"

"Put me on, what happened?"

"A car of guys rode down Fifty-first and Clarkson around nine-thirty this morning, saw Kenyatta, shot him in his chest, and waited till he hit the floor and then got out the car and shot him four times in his head." After they did that, Billy told me, they just started to fire at random. An old man got shot in his leg while getting into his car, and some kid named Shaune also got shot.

Billy seemed like he didn't want to go into details about why it had happened so I didn't ask. Had Kenyatta done something to those guys? I still don't know.

My eyes started to wander and I saw two men in suits walking in and out of the apartment buildings on Fifty-third Street, about two blocks away from the crime scene. Billy noticed what I was looking at and told me the two men were detectives. They had been there since the morning, asking people questions.

"No one is going to tell them anything," was all I could say, because I knew the guys from around the way would want to take care of business themselves.

After that we really had nothing else to say to each other, so we said our goodbyes. Billy hugged me tighter than the first time and told me to get to my friend's house safe.

When I got to the scene of the shooting, the mood was very tense. All the guys I knew were outside smoking weed and drinking forties. It was so weird—everyone was outside and no one was making a sound. Even the cars seemed to be in whisper mode. I didn't speak to anyone because I didn't know what to say.

I rang Nicole's bell and went into her house and waited until she finally got dressed. Then we went outside and there was everybody standing right where I left them—sobbing, hurting, and plotting how to get revenge for their homeboy.

They all had tears in their eyes. Even my ex-boyfriend Flex, a guy who is as hard as a rock, crumbled. When I looked into his eyes I saw fear mixed up with so much hate—he would have sought revenge by any means necessary. That's when I came to the conclusion that I could never really love a gangster because they always love you and leave you and most of the time it's to the barrel of a nine-millimeter.

We stood on the corner for about half an hour and listened to a neighborhood friend named Latoya talk about how she still couldn't believe Kenyatta was dead because she saw him the day before, but you know—here today, gone tomorrow. Nicole and I stood on the corner in silence until a friend of ours named Bell said, "Hey, what y'all doing standing on the corner with a bunch of hoods like us?"

I cracked a little smile for him, but that definitely didn't last too long. "Nothing," I said. "What are you doing out here?"

"Waiting for you to come around." Then he gave me a little smile. But before I could give him my reply, one of his friends called him over. The only thing Nicole and I actually heard Bell's friend say was that nobody was going to come into our neighborhood and disrespect us without getting theirs.

I'm so tired of people who think an eye for an eye is the answer that when Bell walked back over to us I didn't hesitate to tell him, "I'm not going to anyone's funeral, because all of y'all too young to go."

"You don't have to worry about anything," he said. "I'll outlive you. I'm going to be at least a hundred and five years old."

That's wishful thinking. He'll be lucky if he makes it to twenty-five, with the way all these guys out here are taking people's lives with no remorse. It's like the code of the streets—you smoke my homeboy; I'll smoke you. But does this ever solve anything? Don't they see that after they avenge their friend's name, someone will want revenge for the injustice that their friend has been served? And then this vicious cycle continues.

In my experience, all it gets them is either severe battle wounds or a six-foot hole at the local cemetery. I've seen one too many guys die by the hand of steel. It's like they never learn. Whatever happened to good old-fashioned fist-fighting? If you feel you have to correct something, why not have a one-on-one instead of pulling out? As the saying goes, revenge is sweet. But people who believe that should remember that it can also be deadly.

I didn't know Kenyatta that well, so when I cried later that night it really wasn't about him. It was more about me—the sheer fact that I could have been out there that morning. Or it could have been some little kid going to school. I just sat and sobbed uncontrollably, feeling like I had no options and that there would be no end to this cycle of violence.

No one should have to feel the way I felt that night—lonely, hurt, mad, and sad. No one should feel such despair at age seventeen. The death of Kenyatta symbolized something for me. It showed me that the world is really a cold place to be, because after the tears dry up and the bloodstains have disappeared, someone else will die and there will be more blood and more tears.

No one seems to understand why I feel the way I do. People think I'm being melodramatic. But I'm not. I don't want some knuckleheads to decide that because they don't like how I looked at them one day, my time here is done. The deadly game that they play takes innocent lives, and I'm scared the next life they'll take will be my own.

Kenyatta isn't the only person I've known whose life was ended too soon. About a year ago something similar hit even closer to home—a friend of mine was shot and killed while two guys were trying to rob the pharmacy where he worked as a security guard. He tried to close the door on them, but they pushed the gun in and shot him.

My friend was going to school and had three kids he supported. They lost a father and a best friend. Who would have wanted to be the one to tell those kids that two uncaring men took away one of the most important people in their lives? I know I would not have wanted that job.

I don't have any solutions for the violence problem because even though I see what's going on, I feel very helpless. There are people my own age who have no regard for human life. How are things supposed to get better if the teens who are doing the bad deeds don't want to admit there is a problem? No one can help them if they don't accept any help. Not their parents, their teachers, the city, or the state. If they wanted help, they would throw the guns away and start doing positive things like going to school to learn, not fight.

The only things that keep me going are the fact that I'm scared of death (even though I sometimes need to be reminded why I should want to go on living) and my quest to find a place where nothing but happy things exist. Everyone should have a place like that, even if you can only go to that place for five minutes. Maybe if we start giving kids positive reinforcement from the time they're born, we might all have some hope of finding a place like that for the future.

III.

It's Not Black and White

ESSAYS ABOUT RACE AND CULTURE

I Ain't Got No Culture

Lara Coopéy, 17

My friends Maura and Dave are Irish. In fact, they are the two most Irish people I know. Maura has deep red hair and bright blue eyes. Everyone in her family has red hair and blue eyes! Her father even has an Irish accent. Dave's family has an Irish Parking Zone Only sign in their basement. They throw these huge St. Patrick's Day parties every year. They have lots of Irish folk albums around the house, and sometimes when Maura goes over there, she and Dave will do the Irish jig.

Dave and Maura aren't the only people I know with strong cultural identities. My friend Tom was born in India. Whenever I go to his house, I can smell the Indian spices his family cooks with. His parents listen to Indian music and his mom wears a sari all the time.

Then there's Matt and Ellen, who celebrate Greek Orthodox Christmas every year. And my boyfriend, who's always speaking Italian to his mother. In short, go visit any of my friends and you can tell where their families are from practically the moment you walk in the door.

My house is a different story. The only music you'll hear coming out of my parents' stereo is classic rock. The closest thing to a foreign language you'll hear are their strong Brooklyn accents. Instead of having corned beef and cabbage or lasagna for dinner, I have fast food or something out of the microwave. I don't think I'd survive without McDonald's, pizza, and takeout Chinese. Occasionally we'll have steak and mashed potatoes for dinner. Can you get more American than that?

So when people ask me what I am, I don't know what to say. I don't really know where I'm from. Sometimes I think I may have fallen from the sky. Everyone assumes I'm Irish. After all, I look more Irish than anything. But in reality, I'm a mixed breed, a mutt.

My mother's family is Jewish. Her great-grandmother was born in what was then Romania, but now the area is in Poland. My father is Catholic. His great-grandparents were born in France but grew up in Ireland. There's someone from Holland in my family all the way back. Four generations back, I have some relatives who were born in Helsinki, Finland. But our family has lived in America for so long that we have no connection to our homelands at all. We've lost all touch with any relatives we may have in other countries.

I envy the strong connection my friends have to their backgrounds. Even their names (Gilmartin, Ventura) are not just something that people call them but a statement about where they're from. I wish that I had a culture, any culture, to follow. I think that I'm missing out on what it feels like to have a real heritage. When I listen to Maura ramble on for hours about her trips to Ireland, I wish I had a homeland to go back to—other than Brooklyn, that is. Having my Jewish grandmother make mondelbread is about as far as I get.

I guess in a way I might be lucky. Some of my Jewish friends are allowed to date only Jewish guys. They have to lie to their parents if they're seeing anyone outside of their religion. One of my friends attends a Catholic school and has a semi-religious family. When her mom found out she was seeing someone who was Jewish, she flipped out. My parents are very liberal about things like that, considering their own marriage. There's no sense of my having to "stick to my own kind." A lot of my friends envy me for having so much freedom when it comes to that.

Still, I think something's missing from my life. I envy my friends when I see them practicing the different traditions of their cultures. They seem so proud of who they are. I think that all of them have not only a stronger cultural identity than I have but a stronger personal identity too.

Yo, Hollywood!
Where Are the Latinos At?

Jessica Vicuña, 16

I loved the novel *The House of the Spirits* by Chilean author Isabel Allende. When I heard that the movie version was coming to a theater near me, I jumped for joy. I was a little worried that the movie wouldn't be as good as the book, but I pushed those thoughts to the back of my mind. Then I saw Jeremy Irons and Meryl Streep on the movie poster and I really started having second thoughts about the whole thing.

I was right to worry. The movie reeked so badly that I almost wanted to yell, "Fire!" so that everyone could rush out of the theater and save themselves from further disappointment.

What made it so vile were the actors. They couldn't make me believe that they were Chileans. They were white. They didn't even use Spanish accents. What were they thinking?

You see, the movie, like the book, is set in Chile. It's the story of a woman named Clara, whose supernatural powers and good heart capture the love of her husband Esteban, a loving but power-hungry man, and that of his loyal and submissive sister Férula.

The story follows the family into the next generation to show Blanca, the daughter of Clara and Esteban, all grown up and totally in love with Pedro, a peasant who works on her father's plantation. It's about romance but also about politics and history.

By the end of the movie, I heard people in the audience saying, "I didn't know Americans lived in Chile during the roaring twenties."

Of course, I understand how they could make a mistake like that. The characters were so American-sounding that Winona Ryder, who plays Blanca, should've said, "Surf's up" as one of her opening lines.

What I can't understand is why the movie wasn't done in Spanish with subtitles or why the actors couldn't have put on a little accent to indicate that their characters live in South America.

But no, they had to make the movie in English with top-rated American actors who don't look or sound even slightly Hispanic. The worst part was that the only characters who looked authentic were the minor ones—the peasants and the low-wage workers who had no speaking parts.

What kind of image of Hispanics is the movie industry trying to present? Are they saying we're not good enough to play major roles? Are we only good enough for nonspeaking parts that encourage stereotypes of Hispanics as poor and uneducated?

When I was going home after the movie, I started wondering why other ethnic groups don't get treated this way. I mean, the leading roles in *The Godfather* trilogy and *Goodfellas* were played by Italian actors. And the stars of *The Joy Luck Club* and *The Last Emperor* were Asian. But it seems like whenever there's a movie about Hispanics, the directors and producers cast white actors.

It's about time the movie industry gave more work to Hispanic actors, directors, and producers. I'm sorry, but I don't want to see Al Pacino play any more Hispanic roles like the leads in *Scarface* and *Carlito's Way*. In *Carlito's Way*, he's supposed to be playing a street-smart Puerto Rican drug dealer who wants out, but instead he comes across as a trigger-happy dweeb. And Al's attempts to achieve a Puerto Rican accent just make him sound like he has a frog stuck in his throat.

At least in *Scarface* (when he was much younger and more eager) he sounded and carried himself like a Cuban. That's the only movie I can remember where a person who wasn't Latino played a Hispanic character well.

I know it sounds rather harsh saying that only Hispanics should play Hispanic roles, but think how silly the movie *The Last Emperor* would be if Jeremy Irons played the emperor. What if Winona Ryder was one of the daughters in *The Joy Luck Club*? It wouldn't look realistic because they're not Asian, right? So why should movies about Latinos be held to a different standard?

If there were lots of movies being made about Hispanics, then maybe I would feel differently. If Hispanics were always getting good movie roles and got to play white characters, then I'd be okay with whites playing Hispanic roles. But it's just not that way. So for now, only Hispanics should get to play Hispanic roles. I firmly stand by this.

I've felt this way ever since I discovered that a lot of the Puerto Rican characters in *West Side Story* were played by white people (that's not counting the great Rita Moreno). Like the part of Maria: when I found out that Natalie Wood wasn't Puerto Rican and that the guy who played Bernardo was also Caucasian, I flipped. They played their roles well, I'll admit, but their presence made the movie seem so unreal to me. Whenever I saw Maria and Bernardo on the screen, I'd think, "But they're white."

West Side Story was made in the sixties. Isn't it funny how thirty years later movies like *The House of the Spirits* continue to deny Hispanic actors the opportunity to play Hispanic roles?

When I was a kid, every time I finished watching a TV show or a movie, I would sit and wait for all the credits to appear to see if any Hispanics had contributed to the production. I guess I wanted to feel a sense of pride that my people were a part of something as classy and glamorous as the movie industry. Of course I would see a Perez and Gonzalez here and there, but they were usually something like the electrician's helper, never the actors or the producers.

Even though movies and TV exaggerate a lot, they are the mirrors of what society is really all about. When I see Latinos in movies playing drug pushers, addicts, and prostitutes, I can't help wondering if that negative image is all that other people see when they look at us.

If it is, then they have forgotten the many writers, painters, politicians, and singers who have contributed to Hispanic culture. I'd like to see some movies about them for a change. And yes, I'd like those movies to star Hispanic actors.

COLOR ME DIFFERENT

Jamal Greene, 17

I am black. Yet since I was twelve, I've gone to a school almost totally devoid of black people. I don't speak in slang. I don't listen to rap or reggae, and try as I might, I have at best a fifty-fifty chance of converting a lay-up. Except for the fact that I'm not white, I am not all that different from a stereotypical white kid from the suburbs.

Because of this, when I am around other black people, I usually feel a certain distance between us. And so do they. For example, this past summer I took a journalism workshop at New York University. After it was over, I was on the phone with one of the girls in the workshop, a black girl, and we got to talking about first impressions. She said that for about the first week of the workshop, she was saying to herself, "What's wrong with this guy? Is he white or something?" She said that I talked like a "cracker" (as she put it) and she made a lot of offhand remarks about my not being a "real" black person. It irritated me that this girl thought that just because I didn't speak black English, I was not a genuine black person.

I have often heard people criticize Yankee announcer Paul Olden for the same thing. Olden is black, but you would never know it from the way he talks. They say he's trying to be white. I don't "sound black" either, and I'm not trying to be anything but who I am. It's just the way I talk. Black people who speak standard English don't do it because they want to dissociate themselves from other black people but because they grew up hearing English spoken that way.

Just look at the English boxer Lennox Lewis. He's black, but his accent is as British as can be. Is he "trying to be English" and denying his black roots? Of course not. He just grew up around people who had British accents.

I don't dance like a lot of other black people either. I never learned to move my hips and legs the way most kids you see at parties are able to. I lose the beat if I have to move more than two body parts at once, and so my dancing tends to get a little repetitive.

When I go to parties with black people I often find myself sitting at the table drinking a Coke while everybody else is dancing. "Why aren't you dancing?" people ask. And then when I do get on the dance floor, the same people sneer at me. "What's wrong with you?" they say. "Why do you just keep doing the same thing over and over again?"

Contrary to popular belief, black people aren't born with the ability to dance and play basketball. Even though I have speed and leaping ability, I can't drive to the hole without losing my dribble. Those skills have to be learned and perfected with experience. It only seems like they are innate because the black community in America is culturally very close-knit and people share the same interests.

Another thing that constitutes "blackness" in a lot of people's minds is an interest in or a feeling of pride and identification with things historically black. I collected baseball cards until I was fifteen. I had a pretty substantial collection for a kid. At least I thought I did. One afternoon, my cousins came over to my house and were looking at my baseball cards.

"Do you have any Jackie Robinson cards?" one of them asked.

"Of course not," I answered.

They were visibly displeased with that response. Of course in my mind I knew that the reason I didn't have any Jackie Robinson cards was the same reason I didn't have any Ted Williams or Mickey Mantle or Joe DiMaggio cards. I just didn't have the money for Jackie Robinson. Even if I were going to spend that much on baseball cards, I would buy a Mickey Mantle card before I would buy a Jackie Robinson card of the same price. Jackie may have been the first black major leaguer, but Mickey hit home runs and home runs increase the value of baseball cards faster than historical novelty does. It's that simple. But my cousins thought that the reason I didn't have any Jackie Robinson cards was because I didn't like black players as much as white players.

My family has always had a problem with my liking baseball—a game that did not integrate until 1947—as much as I do. They keep getting me Negro League postcards because they are worried that I don't know enough about the subject. And they're right. But then again, sports enthusiasts in general don't know enough about the Negro Leagues. My family feels very strongly that as a black sports fan, I should feel an added responsibility to know about black baseball players. If I don't learn about them, they say, then nobody will.

Minorities are often called upon to be the spokespeople for their races. The only black kid in the class is almost always asked to speak when the subjects of slavery or the civil rights movement come up. The question is, does he have a responsibility to know more about issues pertaining to blacks than his white classmates do? I would like to think that he doesn't.

If we really believe that everyone should be treated equally, then ideally my Jewish friends should be expected to know just as much about black history as I do. Of course I should know more about the Negro Leagues than I do now, but so should a white baseball fan or a Japanese baseball fan or a polka-dot baseball fan.

So I guess I don't fit in with the black people who speak black English, dance with a lot of hip motion, and hang out with an all-black crowd. And I don't feel any added responsibility to learn about black history or go out and associate with more black people either. Nor do I fit in with blacks who like Clarence Thomas: they try as hard as they can to separate themselves from blacks altogether, vote Republican, and marry white women. I'm not like that either.

Even though I grew up playing wiffleball with white kids in Park Slope instead of basketball with black kids in Bed Stuy, even though I go to a school with very few blacks, and even though most of my friends are white and Asian, I can't say that I feel completely at home with white people either. Achieving racial equality is a process that still has a long way to go. Blacks were slaves just one hundred thirty years ago. Until just thirty years ago, we were legally inferior to whites. Blacks may have achieved equality before the law, but it will take another few generations to achieve social equality.

There is still a stigma attached to interracial relationships, for example, both romantic and otherwise. Whenever I'm around the parents of white friends, I get the sense that they see me not as "that nice kid who is friends with my son or daughter" but rather as "that nice black kid who is friends with my son or daughter." There is still a line that certain people are unwilling to cross.

So after all this analysis, I'm still confused about what it means to be black. What is race, anyway? According to *Webster's Dictionary*, race is "a class or kind of people unified by a community of interests, habits, or characteristics."

Well, anyone who's ever called me or any other black person "white on the inside" because we didn't fit his or her stereotype can look at that definition and claim victory. "There it is, right in the dictionary," this person can say. "Black is an attitude, not just a color."

By that definition I'm not black at all. But I was black the last time I looked in the mirror. So I went back to the dictionary and found that *Webster's* has another definition for race: "a division of mankind possessing traits that are transmissible by descent and sufficient to characterize it as a distinct human type."

Wait a minute! Does that mean that a black person is anyone with dark skin, full lips, a broad nose, and coarse hair? These are traits transmissible by descent and distinct to black people. By the second definition, to be black means to have these physical characteristics. Speaking black English and dancing well are not genetic. They are cultural and arise from blacks living in isolation from other communities.

Which definition is right? I would like to think that it is the second. I would like to think that race is nothing more than the color of your skin, but clearly in most people's minds it's more than that. I feel distanced from blacks because I am black but don't act the part, and I feel distanced from whites because I act white but don't look the part. As long as other people expect me to act a certain way because of the way I look or to look a certain way because of the way I act, I will continue to be something of an outcast because I defy their prejudices.

The reality is that I am different from a stereotypical white kid from suburbia because no matter how I act, others will see the two of us differently. Society has different expectations of us and becomes uncomfortable if either one of us strays from those expectations. Just ask anybody who's ever picked me for two-on-two just because I was black.

The "N" Word: It Just Slips Out

Allen Francis, 18

"What's up, niggaz?"

"You crazy nigga, you buggin'!"

"See you later, niggaz!"

That's the way my older brother and his friends used to talk to each other.

I think I was around seven when my older brother became the center of my attention. He and his friends sounded so cool, and that strange, interesting word "nigger" would come up in their conversations so much.

So to be like my older brother and his friends, I made the word "nigger" (or today's preferred spelling, "nigga") a part of my vocabulary. It was how my family and friends addressed each other—seriously, humorously, and otherwise. My brothers, sisters, and I used it freely, and I never thought twice about it.

Even though I used it all the time, the word had no real meaning for me. I just substituted it for phrases such as "What's up?" and "Hey, you."

It wasn't until fourth grade that I learned the racist meaning of the word. A chubby, naive kid named Al asked his teacher, "Is there still prejudice in the South?"

My teacher looked at me, perplexed, and said, "Prejudice is everywhere." That's when I started to take Black History Month seriously and learned about the struggles of Dr. Martin Luther King,

Jr. and all those other prominent figures in the civil rights movement. I saw all those movies and documentaries that showed blacks being whipped, beaten, attacked by dogs and having firehoses opened on them during sit-ins and demonstrations.

It shocked me so, so much that it would take me too long to go into how. And then, in the midst of all the racist violence, I heard that word uttered. It was a white racist speaking down to a black, or talking about blacks, I don't even remember exactly.

But I remember how it sounded. "You nigger" or "those niggers." Even though it was on TV and not directed at me personally, it sounded horrible. I could hear the evil in the word. That's when I understood what it meant. It was a word used to make blacks feel inhuman and worthless.

Still, it wasn't until I was in my mid-teens that I tried to make myself stop saying it. I decided it was wrong for me to use it when it meant such a terrible thing. I didn't try to stop others, I just stopped myself. No one even noticed.

Once, when I was a freshman in high school, we discussed the word in class. The only conclusion we came to was that it was okay for blacks to call other blacks "niggas," but if a white person was unfortunate enough to utter this word to a black person, that white person would be very sorry.

By this point I was very confused about the whole matter. I talked to family and some friends about the situation, but it always came back to the same thing. Black on black was okay, but white on black was a no-no. Gradually, I started using it again.

Maybe peer pressure or everyone else using the word is what brought me back, but I feel that is just an excuse. On some level, I had accepted the word. It was part of me. For better or for worse, using the word "nigga" has become a part of black culture, or at least some segments of it. Now that I don't actively try to stop using the word, it just comes out naturally.

I do still watch who I use it around. I think everyone has a set of rules for when to use the word and when not to, the way many people do with curse words. I use it in my neighborhood and around people I know. I don't use it around people I don't know or who I think might take offense at it, and I try not to use it in professional places.

At least that's what I thought. But then one day, at my internship, I was talking to my friend Frank. Frank is heavily into hip-hop music like me, and wears the latest hip-hop clothing. He also happens to be white. I was talking to him about my neighborhood, and I let the "N" word slip out. Right away, I looked around to see if anyone had heard because I did not want to offend anyone.

What really shocked me was the fact that I had used that blacks-only term in conversation with a white person. I don't know if Frank noticed; if he did, he didn't say so. But I sure felt funny about it.

I had gotten so relaxed talking with a friend about our favorite music that I didn't see his color, maybe because I didn't want to or maybe because it just wasn't important to me at the time. I was talking with my friend, not my white friend. Did that make me a sellout to the race? What the hell was wrong with me?

After that, I was more confused than ever.

It's funny to me that a white calling a black "nigga" is a crime, but sometimes the reverse is accepted. On the single "Award Tour" by A Tribe Called Quest, there is a bonus track called "The Chase, Part II" featuring a rapper named Consequence who says in a verse that he's "been through more *Growing Pains* than that nigga Michael Seaver."

I've also heard some Puerto Ricans at my school use the term—I remember distinctly a Puerto Rican girl referring to her man as "my nigga." And at least some Puerto Ricans I know don't seem to get offended when they are called niggas. Still, part of me continues to think it isn't proper for someone outside the race to use the word. But then I think I may be a hypocrite since I used it so casually when talking to a white person.

And there's still the question of why black people use it to begin with. I wish I knew. Maybe we have decided to take control of this otherwise bad word to use for our own purposes. Maybe we want to give it a new meaning. Or maybe we cling to the word so as to never forget what the black race went through. Maybe it makes us feel good to have become the users of the word and not the victims of it.

As for me, I still go on, monitoring my mouth, hoping for an end to my mixed feelings toward the word, wishing I could either feel completely comfortable using it or banish it totally from my vocabulary. I feel like the rapper Q-tip in the song "Sucka Nigga": "Yo, I start to flinch as I try not to say it, but my lips is like the ooh-wap as I start to spray it."

MY LEBANESE PASSPORT

Mohamad Bazzi, 17

Some people imagine it's exciting to be an immigrant. I've learned to shrug them off. I tell them if they think it's so much fun, they should try going through Immigration and Customs inspections at Kennedy Airport—in my shoes.

My Lebanese passport makes airport officials very nervous. Not only am I Lebanese but I'm a Muslim, and even worse, I'm a Shiite. I'm also a young man so they assume the worst: I must be a religious fanatic waiting to blow up a plane.

"Where's that bomb?" they probably ask themselves. "Come on, kid. Don't waste our time."

Last year I was coming back from visiting my brother who lives in Paris when an official saw my documents and pulled me aside. His colleague asked where I had been. "Paris," I said.

"What were you doing there?" he shot back, as if the concept of a Lebanese immigrant vacationing in Paris defied all logic. I explained, but he still seemed skeptical.

"Do you have anything in there that you shouldn't be carrying?" he asked, pointing to the suitcase.

"Like what?" I asked innocently.

"I don't know. You tell me."

"I don't think so," I answered, unsure if it was a trap.

"Well, let's just check," he said, instructing me to open my bags. So unlike most other travelers (especially American passport holders, who were getting a warm welcome home and breezing right through), I had my bags rummaged through once again.

In a way, I felt violated. Why me? Should I get an American passport and change my name from Mohamad to Michael so that I can get through the inspection more quickly?

These INS and Customs agents are America's way of welcoming its immigrants. It doesn't sound as good as your textbooks make it out to be, does it? No Statue of Liberty on the horizon, no fireworks—just lots of questions and dirty looks.

ASIAN BY ASSOCIATION

Jessica Vicuña, 17

When I first entered Phillipa Schuyler Intermediate School at the tender age of eleven, I was alone and afraid with no one to call my friend.

At first, I tried hard to make friends with kids who were Puerto Rican like me, but they would laugh at me and say that I was "weird" just because I didn't talk with a Brooklyn accent and I dressed in khakis and long preppy sweaters.

The black and Hispanic kids thought I was wack because I didn't dress hip-hop. They considered my outfits "white" attire. I wasn't trying to act white; that was just how I naturally dressed. But the other kids snickered and stared like I was some sort of a freak show. My first month of middle school was hell.

Then one day in homeroom, I saw an Asian girl sitting alone with her head on her desk. She seemed really sad, and no one was talking to her. I wanted to strike up a conversation with her but I didn't have the guts to introduce myself because she seemed pretty pissed off. I didn't get to talk to her until two weeks later when Shatisha, the only person in homeroom who spoke to me, introduced us.

The lonely Asian girl's name was Cindy. We hit it off well from the first conversation. We talked about action movies (*Rambo*, *Showdown in Little Tokyo* and *Kung Fu Masters*) and about how we were both depressed out of our minds. We had the whole school telling us what major herbs we were, and if that wasn't bad enough we had our mothers telling us how ugly we looked and nagging us to dress more feminine.

Cindy and I had more than everything in common: we were soulmates. I thought to myself, "This chick is cool." Within a month we were best friends, inseparable.

Cindy was the first true friend I ever had. Acquaintances I had, but never a real friend, someone who was constantly there for me in my time of need. The fact that she was from a different race didn't matter (even though the only Asians I knew before Cindy were from TV: Bruce Lee and the cartoon cast members of *Voltron*).

I did hold a lot of stereotypes about Asians. I thought they were all computer geniuses with the ability to break their enemies with their bare knuckles. Cindy wised me up: she failed her eighth-grade computer class and she didn't know any kung fu. (For her, the art of self-defense involved one weapon—her mouth.)

I also expected Cindy to tell me stories about traveling to China and meeting a Buddhist monk and reaching enlightenment. Or maybe about leaving the hard times in China and coming to America in search of a happier life but finding out that in America life was still a struggle. But these fantasies were crushed when she told me she was born in the U.S.A. Cindy was an American girl like me; she never talked about her culture except to praise Cantonese cuisine and how perfect it always tastes.

We were friends for five months and I still had never been to her house. I think Cindy was kind of embarrassed to have me meet her family since she wasn't too fond of them at the time.

Finally, during Chinese New Year she asked me if I wanted to go to her house and eat lunch. I nodded my head yes. I wanted to see how the other half lived since she'd been in my house only about fifty times.

As she put the key in the door I imagined her house would just have regular wallpaper, leather sofas, and simple interior decorating mumbo jumbo. But when I walked inside, I saw statues of Buddha, calendars with pictures of famous Hong Kong singers, canvas wall hangings covered with Chinese letters, and tiny red packets lying around everywhere.

I asked her what the red packets were for. She looked around and said, "Oh, that's because next week will be Chinese New Year and it's good luck to have them around the house so you can have a great year." She explained that red symbolized good luck and that there was a little money inside the packets to bring wealth in the new year.

I really wanted to learn more about China after that. I figured if the country's cultural traditions were that interesting, imagine its history. Like the emperors and revolutions and so forth. I was right. I read books about the Xiang Dynasty and the Boxer Rebellion (a war fought to keep Westerners and Christians out of China; it didn't succeed). Because I was so interested in her culture, Cindy became more interested in it than ever before.

Cindy started teaching me how to speak in Cantonese with phrases like "Hello" and "I love you." Her pride and knowledge in her culture was something very new to me. It was a side of her that rarely came out. It was great to see her spend endless hours reading a book of twelfth century poems from the Tang dynasty (which I'd steal from her backpack whenever I got the chance).

She also taught me the basic traditional rules of etiquette among the Chinese people. Like, for instance, how to properly hold and use chopsticks. (Those babies are really slippery to eat with, but Cindy's patience and smiles made up for the long hours of frustration I suffered while learning.) Even dancing in Mandarin old-school style was a great trip for me (understand I didn't join any Mandarin dance team).

I think seeing someone from another culture—me—find something beautiful in Chinese traditions made Cindy appreciate them more. She was the type who, every time she saw a Chinese person speaking fluently in Chinese or listening to Chinese music, would call them F.O.B. (for "fresh off the boat"). Even though she was born here, she feared being tagged as an F.O.B., or hick, herself. I guess that's why she never talked about her culture or took me to her house when we first met.

I was getting into the Chinese culture pretty heavily. I begged my mother to pay for my Cantonese language classes, I only wanted to eat Cantonese food, and I wanted to wear those long silky black Chinese dresses, the ones that drag on the floor. I had never gotten so caught up in anything before. Learning about something because you want to is much better than learning about something because you have to.

Since Cindy, her family, and her friends had accepted me without hesitation I felt comfortable about approaching other Asians. When I met Kim, another close friend who is Chinese, we instantly connected by talking about our favorite music groups and Broadway plays. We also would talk about China and the Tiananmen Square Massacre (when thousands of people were killed after the government ordered the army to put a stop to massive pro-democracy demonstrations in Beijing). The fact that we both knew so much about China made for a special bond between us.

When I met Kathy, another close friend, I asked her if she took any Chinese courses in Chinatown. She told me that she was Vietnamese, not Chinese. Whoops! My mistake didn't offend her, but it made me feel bad anyway. It was like saying all Asians look the same, so they are the same. I wouldn't want someone to just assume that I'm Dominican when, in fact, I'm Puerto Rican.

I don't know why I have so many Asian friends. I can only tell you that I often feel more comfortable with them than I do with other Hispanics. I love my Hispanic culture, don't get me wrong, but when I'm around a bunch of Hispanic people I get nervous because I feel like I have to prove myself. I feel like they won't think I'm Latina enough for them unless I'm speaking Spanish, eating Latin food, and listening to salsa music. I guess I still have bad feelings about my own people because of my experience in junior high school, when I was made to feel like an outcast because of the way I talked and dressed.

These days I'm so surrounded by Asian people and so immersed in Chinese culture that I sometimes feel like I'm more Chinese than Latina. A friend of mine who's into Buddhism thinks that I was Chinese in my former life. Maybe that explains it.

My Journey Home

Anna Song, 18

The number 7 train to Flushing makes a loud, unending noise. On a sunny day, the bright light pours in through the dust-glazed windows, casting a wonderful feeling of warmth and cheerfulness inside. And sitting on the hard, gray bench, I absorb this warmth eagerly.

"Mommy, who's driving this train? I don't see the driver," says a small eight-year-old girl.

"That's because the train is magic," replies the kindly mother. "It can go forward and backward all by itself. Didn't you see that it has no wheels?"

That little girl was me, not too long ago.

That was during my second month in America, and in my innocence I had honestly believed my mother's silly story. It made perfect sense to me then that a subway could be magic.

Moving to America hadn't been easy. I remember my mom telling me again and again of the endless paperwork that had to be done, the hours and hours of standing on long lines in government offices, and months of waiting, hoping, until finally we were in the Korean airport, about to make a move that would affect us all for the rest of our lives.

But I was too young then and can't remember all that stuff, only the heavy tears that fell from my eyes as we said our last goodbyes to my beloved grandmother, the masses of people crowding in the din of the airport lobby.

My younger sister, who was more vulnerable than I, sobbed

quietly as she refused to step on the intimidating escalator she was seeing for the very first time. My father had to carry her on his shoulders so the people behind us wouldn't get too impatient.

I remember also the fear and excitement I felt when I peeked— even after my mother told me not to—through the tiny airplane window, twenty thousand feet above sea level.

I remember feeling groggy and tired but still ecstatic when at last the plane landed at JFK Airport in the middle of a warm August night. We were in America!

There was disappointment the next morning, when, expecting to see sky-high buildings, sleek, zooming automobiles, and tall, blond-haired "American" people, all I saw was a quiet, no-nonsense, no-action neighborhood of small, unimpressive houses. (My family had moved in with a friend in Bayside, Queens, for two weeks.)

But a few days later that disappointment was replaced by marvel and wonder as my family went to Manhattan and was introduced to the real New York City. The breathtaking view put all of us in a state of near-euphoria!

Learning the American way of life, however, was another story— an ongoing, painful, joyous, scary, page-by-page turning process. How did I know that when teachers yelled, "Line up in alphabetical order!" they meant by your last name?

But I learned the English language pretty fast, despite occasional slips. What I hated, though, were those first few months when kids came up to me in a slow, cautious way (what did I do?) to say something like, "Hi-An-na-we-go-ing-to-lunch-now, do-you-know-where-it-is?" And they would point almost frantically down to the first floor, where the cafeteria was.

I gave them a slightly shocked, slightly disgusted look. My God—it was December already! I knew some English, and where the lunchroom was besides!

That December brought a lot of firsts: the first school picture, the first "professional" haircut, the first taste of deliciously sweet

Hershey's Kisses. (I had thought they were some kind of metallic-type garlic!)

And, of course, the first Christmas. Wow—what a Christmas! I'm not even sure if my younger brother and sister and I understood what Christmas was all about.

Nevertheless, all of us bubbled with excitement as the family prepared for the festival. We sang "O Christmas Tree" and "Jingle Bells" in front of our oh-so-proud parents. We filled our stomachs with all kinds of goodies, including Korean cakes, the kind that our mom always makes on special occasions.

On Christmas Day we waddled in pure happiness among ripped gift wrappings and odd presents. (How I loved my big, "difficult-to-read" fairy tale book!)

Never mind that there was no warm, crackling fire to sit by, or even a fireplace where Santa could deliver his presents. (He found us anyway.) Who cared that the Christmas tree was a little warped, a little on the "unglamorous" side? It was a beautiful Christmas.

Time flies. The last snow melts and finally evaporates into the air, leaving only a faint remnant of the dirt it picked up a long time ago. People are putting away their heaviest coats, saving them nicely, to be used again next winter. And the boldest flowers awake, blooming to their fullest, dying shortly after. Spring is just days away.

A little girl is walking happily from school. It is Friday and she can't wait to go home. She wants to tell everyone that she just got her first 100 on a spelling test.

Suddenly, two big boys stop in front of her, blocking the little girl's path. They are on bicycles. One of the boys, the one with the bright red hair, starts shifting his bicycle.

The little girl is afraid. She doesn't understand why they are bothering her. What did she do? She wants them to go away, leave her alone!

"Hey, you! What are you doing here, huh? Why don't you go back to China?" the redhead bellows.

"Yeah," the other one follows, "you speak English!"

The little girl doesn't say anything. She's too afraid. She wants to run away, but the bikes are still in front of her.

"Why do you have funny-lookin' eyes?"

"Why don't you speak English?"

"What's your name, huh? Ching-Chong? Sheng-Meng?"

The little girl is running now. The tears in her eyes barely allow her to see where she's going, but she doesn't care. She can still hear the boys laughing, finding her fear hilarious. She just wants to go home, where it's safe.

She never did tell anyone about the 100 on her spelling test.

Every time I used to think of that incident, my cheeks flushed and I'd feel so low and humiliated. But now there's only a dull anger. Those boys were ignorant jerks and didn't know much better. But they gave me my first taste of prejudice in America, and I guess that had to come sooner or later.

Later that day, after a good cry, I remember looking at myself in the mirror and seeing—I mean really seeing— that I was different from most of the kids in school. I had black hair instead of blond, dark brown eyes instead of cornflower blue.

What I'm trying to say is that I realized for the first time that America was not like Korea. Not everyone had the same color hair or eyes. There was bound to be some resentment, some misunderstanding.

My father once told me, "You don't have to feel less important or special because some idiot can't see that my daughter is just as good as another man's daughter. Be proud that you are a Korean!"

And I think that I am. I like the fact that I can speak two languages and am learning two others, that I have a special homeland back in Korea, and a wonderful family that won't ever let me forget who I am.

The subway jerks to a stop, causing some standing passengers to lose their balance and appear self-conscious. A scratchy, nasal voice announces, "There's a slight technical problem, we should be moving shortly."

A few people let out a small, annoyed sigh, I among them. Others give a quick glance at their watches or appear oblivious that anything has happened.

In the far left corner of the subway compartment hangs a large poster that reads, "Lotto Made Our American Dream Come True." And there's a picture of about twenty immigrant men.

Ha! That's a good one. My family came to America, traveled all that distance, so we could spend good money on some silly lottery game that would make our "American Dream" come true? Okay, and I bet we also came to see how it feels to be stuck in a New York City subway—maybe even to read one of these ridiculous advertisements in the meantime.

The train is moving now, and the loud, unending noise begins again. Not bad. It was only a ten-minute delay.

What to look forward to once I reach home, sweet home? Well, for one thing, taking off my shoes and lying down on the sofa. My feet are killing me! Then I'll probably click the radio on to my favorite station, head for the kitchen, grab some potato chips, and head back to my room. Maybe I'll want to fill my head with junk instead and watch some TV.

The point is, who knows what I'll do? I'm just glad the train is moving...

Sometimes I wonder, "What would I be like had I never moved to America? Would I be happier in Korea? What would I be doing every day? Would I even have the same goals?"

Two years ago, my sister and I revisited Korea. We saw every one of our relatives. (I didn't know we had so many!) We saw the good, the bad, the dirty, and the beautiful parts of Korea. We met our cousin, who in our childhood days had been just like us. Yet when we talked and giggled and compared our lives, she wasn't so much like us anymore.

Soon the scratchy, nasal announcement: "Main Street, Flushing. Last stop, everybody off!"

That is my signal. I pop a fresh piece of gum in my mouth, put away the blank papers I'm holding (I thought I was going to do a little writing in the subway), and stand up. It was a long ride, but I am finally going home.

IV.

He Said, She Said

ESSAYS ABOUT GENDER AND SEXUALITY

SINGLE AND LOVIN' IT

Latrice Davis, 17

When I was a child I always looked forward to becoming a teenager because then I wouldn't have to put up with my parents anymore and I'd finally reach high school—the time when I'd get my first boyfriend, go on my first date, get my first kiss, and if I was real lucky, I'd lose...well, you get the idea.

I'm seventeen and none of that has happened to me yet, but I'm actually glad.

For a long time, I thought that if you didn't have at least one boyfriend by the time you were in high school, then something was wrong with you. Now that I've grown older and wiser, I realize that there's more to life than dating.

Being boyfriendless is a big plus in my life right now, because as a high school senior, I'm involved in extracurricular activities, I'm trying to keep my average above 85, and I'm also looking for a part-time job. I know that I wouldn't be able to devote a lot of time to a relationship.

I also treasure my freedom. And although a boyfriend wouldn't take that away from me (I wouldn't let him), my ability to do whatever I pleased, whenever I pleased, would be limited.

Besides taking up a lot of your time, having a boyfriend can be risky. Right now, I know at least five girls who are either pregnant or have already had a baby. I'm sure that if they didn't have a boyfriend in the first place, they wouldn't be in this predicament now. In a lot of ways I'm still a child. And if I can barely take care of myself, then I know that I'm not ready to take care of a baby.

Another problem with dating is that it can ruin a perfectly good friendship. Late in my junior year of high school, I decided to ask Felipe (not his real name) out on a date. I knew him for a while, and not only was he cute (not all that, just cute), he also had a nice personality.

I hesitated for a few days about doing it, but I finally decided that it was okay for a girl to ask a guy out. (This is the age of feminism, isn't it?) I had a feeling he was going to turn me down, but I decided to go ahead and do it anyway because if I didn't, then I would never know his answer.

As I expected, he said no, telling me that he had a girlfriend. Since I can handle rejection, I didn't make a big deal out of it. But ever since then we don't hang out like we used to and I feel a little awkward whenever I'm around him. Although Felipe and I are still friends, our friendship just isn't the same anymore.

For the most part, the people I know don't knock me for not having a boyfriend, but there are a few exceptions. My mother, for example, is always bugging me about it. On any particular Saturday night, she'll say, "Tricey, when I was your age, I used to have boyfriends galore. My mother didn't know what it was like to see me at home on a Saturday night." Like I really care what she did thirty years ago.

I'm not ashamed to tell people that I've never had a boyfriend, but I hate it when they make assumptions about my social life (especially when they don't know anything about me). Over the summer, the boyfriend of a friend of mine asked me if I had a boyfriend of my own. Since I had nothing to hide, I said no (although I was curious as to why he wanted to know in the first place).

Right away, he started to bombard me with questions: "How come?" "Are you attracted to men?" And the ultimate question, "Are you a lesbian?'"

I've always felt that whatever I did in my bedroom was my

business, and since he's never been there (and he won't ever be going there), neither he nor anyone else, for that matter, should care.

Over the years, it has become more difficult for me to have friends without having one of them try to play matchmaker for me. Recently, my friend Josie (not her real name) was shocked to learn that I'd never been kissed. "I know that you've never had a boyfriend, but you've never been kissed?" she said. "What a shame; I need to hook you up with a man."

Some people just don't get it. I'm not in any rush. I don't need all the headaches that come along with having a boyfriend right now. Besides, it's not as if I don't know where to go or what to do if I ever wanted one. I wish that people would stop worrying about my love life and concentrate on their own (if they have one to begin with).

Don't get me wrong, I'm sure that having a boyfriend can be a wonderful thing, but it requires a commitment that I can't offer right now. A lot of girls seem to think that they need a man in order to feel secure or to be accepted. I may decide I want a boyfriend someday, but I don't need one. I love myself, I respect myself, and I can most certainly take care of myself. If people would just accept me as being proudly boyfriendless, my life would be a lot less stressful.

DREAM GIRL

Rance Scully, 19

*I*t was summer. School was out, and my friends and I decided we were going to start hanging out with more girls. None of us understood anything about them. So we took it upon ourselves to go and find out what they were really like. Don't get me wrong, this wasn't one of those competitions to see who could get the most girls over the summer. Our strategy was to try and be their friends and see what we could learn.

Of the four of us, I was the shyest. I made several attempts at striking up conversations, but none of the girls I wanted to talk to wanted to speak to me. They behaved as if the only reason I would talk to them was in order to "get some." It was like a crime to be seen talking to any guy who lived in the neighborhood.

Meanwhile, my friends were having the same experience, and after a week or so, it was obvious that this plan of ours was getting us nowhere. Then one day we were hanging out in front of my house when a group of people got out of a car right across the road. Among them was one of the most attractive girls that I had ever seen.

She had jet black hair, a cocoa butter complexion, and eyes that glittered in the brightness of the sun. She didn't seem to have lipstick on, but her lips had this cherry red color about them.

My friends and I all stared at her in awe until she disappeared into the house across the road. For the rest of the day the only thing we spoke about was how pretty she was and how badly we wanted to get to know her. One of my friends said she looked exactly like his "dream girl."

All at once, I started to regret not having been more friendly with the people who lived in that house. In the weeks that followed, I started to see her moving in furniture. I found myself walking by the house just to try and get a glimpse of her. Each time I saw her, I would end up thinking about her for the entire day. I became obsessed.

Soon my friends were teasing me, asking me, "What's up, Rance? Are you in love with this girl?" I would laugh and try to change the subject, but no matter how hard I tried I just couldn't get over talking about her whenever I got the chance.

I really wanted to meet this girl, but I was too shy to approach her. I would stand in front of my mirror and go over hundreds of things that I would say to her if I ever got the chance. Soon she became the only thing on my mind and I even stopped hanging with my friends. Instead I would sit in my room and draw pictures of hearts and write love letters to her.

My friends called me a coward and threatened to stop hanging with me if I didn't go and talk to her. But I could never seem to gather up the courage.

Then one day when the summer was over and I was on my way home from school, I deliberately walked on the side of the road where she lived and saw a guy talking to her. To my surprise it was Paul the Player. Paul was this guy who drove a real fancy car and had a new girl in it every day. Every girl living in the vicinity knew what he was after. Why was she talking to him?

At first I wondered if maybe no one had warned her about Paul, but I figured that she ought to be smart enough to see straight through his act.

The next day when I was coming home I saw her talking to yet another guy who was famous for his promiscuous behavior. I started thinking that she must be a chickenhead.

But when she started hanging with some of the girls on the block with similar reputations to Paul and the other guy, I decided she wasn't stupid; she must be like them. My heart was broken, and yet I had to think realistically. After all, she wasn't my girlfriend. She was free to do whatever she wanted with herself.

I tried my very best to get her off my mind, and after a few weeks I found myself thinking less and less of her. Then one day I was on the bus and almost like a dream she came on board. The only available seat was the one next to me and without hesitation she sat down in it.

I was uncomfortable. I didn't want to have anything to do with her. "Why is this girl sitting beside me?" I thought to myself, as I slowly turned to get a better look at her. I remember being surprised all over again to see how smooth and spotless her skin was, how beautiful she was. I turned my head and stared out the window.

"Why is it that I have always wanted to speak to this girl," I thought, "and it's only now when I am the least interested that she is sitting right here next to me?" While these thoughts were racing through my head, I kept looking out the window. Then I heard a voice: "Hi," she said.

"Hello," I replied nervously.

"Are you the guy who lives on my block?"

I was surprised to find out that she had even noticed me at all. "Yes," I said.

"What's your name?"

"Rance," I said in a suave and sophisticated manner.

"Unusual, but nice," she said. Her name was Kai and she was being awfully friendly. I was suspicious and wondered to myself whether this friendliness had gotten guys like Paul the Player everything they wanted. But as we continued to talk I started to feel more and more at home with her. She told me where she was from and how her mom was ill and in the hospital for a few months, which was why she was living in Brooklyn.

Before I knew it we were talking like close friends. All this time, I couldn't help admiring her face, especially her lips.

"Are you this friendly to everyone?" I asked awkwardly. She said she was. "Why?" I asked her.

She smiled. "The only way you can know anything about another person is to converse with them," she said. "If you don't like what you hear, stop talking to them."

I looked at her and nodded in agreement. I thought I had this girl all figured out, but once I actually spoke to her, she turned out to be completely different from what I thought. We talked until we got to our stop, and after we got off I walked her to her house and bid her a friendly goodbye.

It wasn't long before she moved out of the neighborhood, but even though we eventually lost touch, we continued to talk on the telephone for a while after that. What began as a big crush turned to suspicion and disdain and then to undying admiration. I suppose I did make a female friend after all—a close one. Kai, if you happen to read this, thanks.

TIRED OF BEING A TARGET

Loretta Chan, 18

On August 3, at 3:30 p.m., some jerk threw a Snapple bottle at me while I was crossing a Manhattan street. I don't know what provoked him—I didn't even know who he was.

When I turned back from the curb where the bottle had landed (thank God it didn't hit me), all I saw was a group of guys standing around, smiling and saying, "Look at her, look at her." When I turned back in the direction I was originally heading, a guy said to me, like it was funny or something, "Baby, somebody doesn't like you."

And I just continued walking to the train station like nothing had happened. At least I acted like nothing had happened. But, behind my sunglasses, I was trying hard not to cry.

I had never felt so defenseless against anyone. It caught me off guard and I couldn't do anything to protect myself or to retaliate. For that moment, I wasn't the I-am-woman-hear-me-roar girl that a lot of people know me as. Instead, I became one of those pitiful girls who can't stand up to a male chauvinist pig. I had never walked away from a situation like that before without at least giving the guy a cold stare and letting him know that I was offended. But all I did this time was walk away like I couldn't care less about how I was treated.

I was on my way to an interview for a summer job and all I could think about was whether this incident was going to make me late.

When I finally got to the train station, a lady told me that my leg was bleeding and handed me some tweezers. A piece of glass had gotten stuck in my leg when the bottle crashed into the curb. Great, I thought, now my interviewer would not only see that my eyes were red, but I would also be bleeding all over his office.

Trying to get the glass out of my leg made me half an hour late for my interview. Still, my main concern was whether or not I would get the job, not why some man I didn't know decided to throw a bottle at me.

Well, I got the job, but I couldn't get the Snapple bottle incident out of my mind. At home that night I told my mother about what happened. I was expecting her to comfort me. Instead, she barely even looked up from her desk. The first thing she said to me, in her Chinese accent, was, "Because of what you wearing. It's too sexy." She even used the same hand gesture she uses when she yells at me for coming home late. She never even said that she felt bad about what had happened. No "Poor baby. Are you okay? Let me get you some milk and cookies." And for the next week, she inspected the way I dressed even more closely than before.

By now you're probably wondering what I was wearing that day. It was a long, sleeveless floral dress that was almost down to my ankles. Okay, it was a little fitted, and had a slit on the side, but in no sense was it "slutty" or "showy" compared to what a lot of other girls were wearing on that hot day.

And what difference does it make? No matter what I was wearing, why should my mother blame me for getting a bottle thrown at me? He was the one who had attacked me. Why did I always have to feel like I was on the defensive whenever I stepped out of the house?

Long before this, I'd learned how to stare straight ahead when passing any male and to walk very quickly. And the other basic stuff: never to get into an empty elevator alone with a guy and not to walk alone in a deserted area at night. But I never thought that anybody would ever attack me on the street, in broad daylight, as long as I minded my own business.

My mind became filled with hateful, violent thoughts towards men. I thought of the remarks from strangers on the street about my body. I thought of those disgusting men who exposed themselves to me on the train. I thought about the perverts whispering their sexual fantasies to me as they passed me or were walking behind me. I had dealt with those things just by putting them out of my mind. But I couldn't just forget the Snapple incident. As the disgruntled say, *"I'm mad as hell and I'm not going to take it anymore!"*

So I started considering other options. First I thought of different ways of cursing guys out. Then I went down to the store to get a bottle of pepper gas. A week later I was looking at stun guns on Forty-second Street. And for a moment I considered getting a small handgun and going to a shooting range to learn how to use it.

I wondered what would have happened to Mr. Snapple if I'd had something with me that day. I don't think I would have attacked him, especially if he was with a group of friends. But maybe I would have had the guts to curse the hell out of him, knowing that I was armed. Then again, maybe not. If he had thrown a bottle at me just because I was there, what would he have done if I really provoked him by fighting back?

As a result of the Snapple incident, I've come to believe something that I've always denied—that women are, in general, more vulnerable than men. Though men have to be on guard for danger wherever they go, they still have a sense of security knowing that they might be a match for another male. Plus, they aren't attacked as often as females are. We simply make easier targets—we might as well have bull's eyes emblazoned on our bodies.

And we are constantly reminded that we are in danger: people warn us that we shouldn't be taking the train at night alone or at all, that we shouldn't be walking down a deserted street after dusk, that there are certain areas a young lady should never wander through.

However, men can roam the entire earth with minimal caution.

What really kills me is that I'm back to square one. I hate spending all this time bitching about something that half of our population has to put up with and not even have a solution. It would be too cheesy just to end with a moral for the males like: Have respect for women. It's such a simple rule of thumb, yet they've had difficulty with it for centuries.

It would be even worse for me to tell other women that we'll just have to put up with abuse and harassment for the rest of our lives. I refuse to accept as a fact of life that males are going to continue treating women this way. Just the thought that women in the future, maybe my own daughters, will be treated as second-class humans makes me want to shred every male on this planet to pieces. In this moment of passion and fury, that's the only solution I can seem to conjure up.

I also know I'm probably not going to physically attack the next man who pinches my butt or makes a lewd comment. So what else can be done? Maybe it begins with a lecture to a dirty old man on the street about how you didn't appreciate the crude remark he just made. Yes, it takes guts. It'll take even more guts to work up from the dirty old man to the construction worker or the group of hoods on the corner. And unfortunately, there will be times when you'll just have to use your common sense and hold back from spitting fire because of what might happen afterward as far as your safety is concerned.

It's driving me crazy that I don't have a better solution to this problem, especially since I know I'm going to be facing it again in just a couple of minutes, when I go outside. Because as far as those dirty old (and young) men out there are concerned, I've still got a bull's eye emblazoned on my body.

A GIRL TAKES CONTROL

Troy Sean Welcome, 19

I was walking down the street with my best friend a couple of months ago when he slipped on a mountain of snow and almost fell down. I started laughing, he started laughing, and a group of girls from across the street started laughing.

We kept walking, but one of the girls called out, "You in the all-black, come here!"

We couldn't see what they looked like because the street corner they were standing on was very dark. After thinking it over, we decided to go and see.

"You look mad good," a husky, dark-skinned female blurted out. She reminded me of Sergeant Slaughter.

"Damn, this girl looks rough," I was thinking. She wasn't even cute. I was speechless. "Word?" I said.

One of her friends, a short-haired, dark-skinned girl, said, "I'm sayin', she was watching you from when you was down the block, so I think y'all should just say y'all words."

I was double shocked. I couldn't believe that I was actually having to take in the words that I was used to dishing out. And it didn't stop there.

"You got a girl?" Sergeant Slaughter anxiously asked.

"Not really," I said.

"You got a commitment?" she countered.

I told her that I didn't, but for the life of me, I don't know why.

Probably because I love to flirt.

Then she asked for my number, but neither one of us had a pen. Unfortunately one of her friends did. I didn't feel like dissing her, so when she asked again, I gave her a number. It wasn't mine, but I'm sure it was somebody's.

There were a couple of reasons why I gave her a wrong number. First of all, she wasn't my type at all. I mean, she looked like she could kick King Kong's butt. The other thing that bothered me was how she talked to me.

It was a weird feeling to be talked to in the same way that I'd sometimes talk to a girl. I was intimidated by the way she spoke to me. I am accustomed to being in control when I'm trying to talk to a girl or she's trying to talk to me, but this girl was dropping line after line on me. I didn't have enough time to think. I didn't like that at all.

You see, we guys love to be in control. It's our nature to plan how we're going to get a female and imagine we're the ones making all the decisions. We don't realize that women know what they're doing too.

My friend Jeanette says, "We [girls] could get y'all [guys] to do whatever we want...we're always a step ahead of y'all guys." But even if that's true, girls usually let us go on thinking we're the ones in control.

Sergeant Slaughter didn't bother to do that. She just came right out and told me what she wanted.

As horrid and dominating as she was, being stopped by her boosted my ego. Girls are always being flirted with in the streets and probably get tired of it. But for me, that was the first comment I'd gotten all day, so I flirted with her a little. The experience made me feel mad good about myself, like I was the man, like I was mad phat. A girl, on the other hand, probably wouldn't think of it in that way. She gets so many comments a day that she probably thinks more about her safety than her ego. I suppose that's what draws the line between guys and girls.

I HATED MYSELF

David Miranda, 17

*B*y the time I was eleven, I already knew I was gay and I hated myself for it. I hated myself so much that I wanted to kill myself. I wanted to be "normal." I didn't want God to punish me and give me AIDS. I didn't want to go to Hell.

Every day after school I would go to church. "Please give me the strength to change myself," I would pray. "Please, please, please." I always expected God to answer me but She or He never did. I remember one day at school one of the kids in my class asked a teacher, "Does God always answer your prayers?" The teacher replied, "Yes, no matter what, in one form or another, God will always answer your prayers." Not mine.

I even made a vow that if God would make me heterosexual I would become a priest. After church I would go home and read the entire Bible. All I remember about being eleven is praying. Every Saturday I went to confession. I would confess everything except that I had gay feelings. On Sundays I made sure I went to mass. None of it worked.

"Why me?" I'd ask myself over and over again. I saw myself as a freak of nature, a devil. All that I ever knew about gay men at the time were the stereotypes and lies that my parents taught me: that they were child molesters and wanted to be women.

"*Siéntate bien,*" my father would tell me. "*Camina como hombre.*" ("Learn how to sit right. Walk like a real man.") He said these things to me so many times that I can still hear him.

My parents taught me that gay people were not people at all. Driving through the West Village I remember them laughing at the *maricas*, and trying to imitate gay people by saying *"Ay, chus,"* and acting like stereotypical homosexuals. This taught me that gay people didn't deserve any respect. So how was I supposed to feel when I discovered that I was gay? How is one supposed to feel when you find out that you are a freak, a pervert, a piece of human sh-t?

One day I told my friend, John (not his real name), that I was planning to kill myself. I asked him how I should do it. "Why don't you try mothballs?" he said. John was supposed to be my best friend. I figured that if my best friend didn't care whether or not I died, then no one would. I knew that I was alone and that there was no one I could turn to. I was scared of people.

That's when I made up my mind to do it. I was scared and felt I didn't deserve to live. It was as if there were a knife lodged in my chest that I couldn't take out. I thought about different ways to kill myself. I went to my roof and looked down, but I was too scared to jump. I figured that Windex could kill a person, so I drank a whole bottle. It didn't even make me sick.

Then I decided to swallow a whole bottle of Tylenol. I drank it down with iced tea, and every time I took another pill I felt glad that I was that much closer to death and that much farther from having to live a miserable life. I closed my eyes and went to sleep hoping it was all over and I'd never have to wake up again.

All I remember from that night was waking up in the darkness every half hour to throw up. I felt as if there was some monster inside of me that just wanted to come out. I remember leaning over the toilet bowl and feeling dirty, and hearing my father say, "Let it out, let it out, you'll feel better." But I just kept throwing up over and over again.

The next morning when I opened my eyes, I felt as if I had spent a night in Hell. I realized that nothing had changed. I still had to deal with my stepmother, who was always hitting me, and on Monday I'd have to deal with the idiots at school again who always brought up the word "f--got."

I went to a guidance counselor and, without telling her that I was gay, told her what had happened. I made up a story about a friend dying. By that time I already knew that the best way to keep my secret was by lying.

The counselor called my father and he rushed to school. She told me to step outside while she talked to him. I waited anxiously, wondering what my dad would do when he came out.

Instead of yelling at me, my normally grumpy father was nicer than I'd ever seen him before. "You're my son and I love you," he told me. "Why would you do something so stupid?" You could tell that he was trying to do everything in his power not to upset me. In a way I was glad because he was giving me a lot of attention. He took me out to eat and talked about moving out of New York City. But in another way it was so fake that it made me uncomfortable.

The guidance counselor told him that I needed to go to the hospital because there was a possibility that the Tylenol could have done physical damage. At least that was the excuse that they gave me to convince me to go to a psychiatric hospital for three months.

I will never forget the fears that went through my mind when they told me I would have to go to a mental hospital. I imagined a place full of crazy people who would try to hurt me. I also imagined a deranged psychiatrist who would put doses of harmful medication in my food.

It turned out that the three months that I spent at the hospital were actually fun. I woke up every morning and went to group meetings and activities. It was the first time that I actually had friends. Up to that time I had tried my hardest to avoid other people my age. I felt that nobody would like me. I hated people.

At the hospital I was with people who actually liked me. They were all older, about sixteen or seventeen, and to them I was the cute little kid. I enjoyed the way they were treating me. During meals we would talk and I would laugh. I know that doesn't sound like much, but laughing and being happy were rare for me in those days. At the end of each day we would go to the gym and work out. It was all a lot of fun. And my parents were nicer to me than they had ever been before.

After three months I was out of the hospital. I had lied my way through the whole therapy, saying that my only problems were my best friend who had committed suicide, the fact that I had no friends, and that I hated myself. The one time the subject of homosexuality came up I just said, "It's weird. I don't understand how anyone cannot like women." They believed everything and then sent me to live with my mother in Brooklyn.

In Brooklyn I found new friends. I continued to live a lie, however. One day I went home and swallowed another bottle of Tylenol, for no reason other than to make myself suffer through another hellish night. Another time I took twenty of my mother's blood pressure pills. I felt that I had no reason to live. My vision of myself as an adult was as a lonely miserable person who would never be accepted by society. The idea of dying in my sleep was very attractive.

I would go to school and chill with my friends and we'd lie to each other about how many girls we'd had. I got into a lot of fights because at that age kids would call each other "f--got." I would get extremely offended by this word, and I would beat up anyone who said it to me. Some of my friends would ask me, "Why do you get so offended when people call you f--got if you know you're not?"

I would ask myself: How did they know what I was or was not? I was still afraid to admit to myself that I was gay. I started asking girls out and lying to myself by telling myself that girls were my thing. I started to date them and I enjoyed it. I enjoyed them as far as friendship was concerned, but I didn't see it going beyond that.

Junior high school was a total flop for me. I did everything to prove my manhood. I stole cars, picked fights, and went on rampages in the train, "catching herbs" with older kids and cutting school. I went from the class nerd to the most likely to drop out.

I got out of it all when I decided to go to a high school that was outside my neighborhood. All of my "friends" were going to the neighborhood high school, so I now had the chance to go and make some new friends in a place where nobody knew anything about me.

On my first day a question was haunting me: "What if people find out?" I was terrified out of my mind.

At first I made many friends, but then I would close up and stop talking to them. I was so afraid of being found out that I would stop going to school just so that I didn't have to deal with people. When I did go I started monitoring my every move. I would be scared to talk, walk, or even look at anyone. I felt as if I had the word "f--got" stamped on my forehead.

Eventually I was put in "holding power," which is a nice way of saying truant class. I was just waiting for my sixteenth birthday so that I could drop out.

It was during high school that I found that I needed a place to meet other gay people. I knew there were places like that out there, but I didn't know how to get in touch with them. I decided that I was going to ask a guidance counselor for places to go. I wasn't sure whether it was the right thing for me to do. I kept thinking about it for weeks. What if he called my parents? What if he laughed at me? What if they threw me out of school?

Finally I arranged to talk with a guidance counselor. My heart raced and my palms were sweaty as I prepared to tell the first person ever about my big secret.

"How can I help you?" Mr. Smith, my guidance counselor, asked me.

"I have a very big problem," I said. Then came the big bomb: "I think I might be gay."

He just smiled and said, "And?"

My first thought was, "Is this a joke?"

All at once I was relieved and shocked to find that the first person I told didn't freak out. The experience gave me a lot of confidence. It helped me to realize that I was being too hard on myself.

Mr. Smith told me about the Hetrick-Martin Institute for Gay and Lesbian Youth. At HMI they had an after-school center where I met other gay and lesbian teens. I couldn't believe that there were other people out there who were going through the same thing I was.

At Hetrick-Martin I got to know kids from all over the city, and of all races. It didn't matter that everyone was gay. What mattered was that everyone was cool. It was a place where I didn't have to hide who I was and where I could just be myself.

At first I kind of felt uncomfortable being around other gay people. The trouble was that after pretending to be somebody else for so long, I really didn't know who I was. The only thing I had thought about since I was eleven years old was what was I going to do about this gay sh-t. At fourteen, I didn't know how to think about anything else.

Then I found that I was not only gay, I also liked to have fun. I liked to go to the movies. I liked to hang out and chill with my friends, and I loved to listen to music. I was smart. I liked to do things that anybody else liked to do. I was a human being just like everybody else; I just happened to be gay. I didn't admit that to myself until I was fourteen.

It was around this time that I started my first relationship. His name was Chris. I met him at HMI and I found that I liked talking to him. We would hang out with our friends, go to clubs, or just chill and talk. I found that with Chris I felt happier than I had ever felt with any girl. Our relationship was totally based on friendship and respect.

Through all of this I was still cutting school and my mom would get suspicious about my hanging out late at night. Sometimes I would come home high on an acid tab and try to act as if I weren't high. I didn't care anymore about school. My only concerns became clubs, my friends, and hanging out.

Finally my mother got fed up with everything and kicked me out of my house and sent me to my father's house. She told me I would amount to nothing and that I would be a bum when I grew up.

I hated my father's house. He would put so many restrictions on me that I wasn't used to. I had to be home by 11:30 p.m. If I wasn't home my father would yell and scream and let me have it. I hated having to put up with that. It was around this time that I was trying to let my parents know that I was gay. I was fed up with living a lie.

One day I arrived home and my father was sitting on the couch watching TV. It was a Friday night and it was only 10:30. "Where were you?" my father yelled.

"I was out," I told him.

"What were you doing?"

By this point I was quite angry. I mean, who did this man think he was to be screaming on my time? I wasn't a little kid, and I was sick and tired of him telling me how to act, what to do, when to do it, and with whom. So I told him that it was none of his business where I was and that he should stay the hell out of my life. That got him very upset.

All of a sudden he grabbed me. "Damn it, you're my son," he said, "and I want to know what you're doing." He started to cry and demanded I tell him if I was using drugs, if I had a girlfriend, a job? But the question that really hurt me was, "Are you a f--got?" It wasn't so much the question itself as the way he asked me. He had the most hateful look on his face, as if he were literally ready to kill someone.

"Let me get the hell out of this house," I yelled. "I don't want to live here anymore."

"You're not leaving this house until you tell me what you're up to," he said.

"Let me go or I swear I'm going to jump out of that window," I replied. The only problem was that the window was five stories up, and I meant what I said.

He started to grab me and hit me. I was screaming and telling him that I was going to kill him. I was actually very scared. He kept telling me to shut up because the neighbors were listening. I told him I wanted them to hear. I wanted to kill him. I wanted to open the door and leave, but he wouldn't let me.

My heart was beating fast and I was gasping for air and crying. I pushed him away, ran for the window, opened it, and was ready to jump, when my father grabbed me. He became very afraid for me, and he said that he was very sorry, and begged me to forgive him. I said that it was all right.

The next day was Saturday and my father called me from his job and told me in a really nice way that in the afternoon we were going to the doctor. I asked why. "You know, just to get a checkup," he said. Later in the day he came to pick me up.

When we walked into the office the doctor asked me, "So what's the problem?"

"This ain't a doctor," I thought. "This is a therapist." I was upset that my father had lied to me and afraid that I would have to spend more time at the hospital. The doctor recommended to my father that I be admitted to Jacobi Hospital. Once I got there they took a lot of blood from me, and then locked me up in a glass room with this man who smelled really bad and who kept talking to himself. Then they gave me this nasty food.

Later they made me talk to a social worker. He kept asking me what was wrong, but I wouldn't tell him. I didn't tell him anything, but he still felt that he had the right to tell my father that he thought I was gay.

After a few hours I was sent to another hospital in the Bronx just for teens and then, after about a week, transferred back to the hospital I had been in when I was twelve. My father and mother would talk to me about how much they loved me and how they would support me in anything I did.

I felt angry and confused because I had never told them anything or officially "come out" to them—someone else had. I felt bad that my parents had to go through all this. I knew they were sad and that they didn't want me to be gay. To be honest, if I had a choice I would not have chosen to be gay either. Who in the world would choose to go through all the name calling, all the bashings, and all the other crap gay people have to go through every day?

In a way I was glad that my parents found out while I was in the hospital because I didn't have to go through the coming-out experience by myself. I had social workers and other people there for me. We would have family therapy where they would put my mother, father, and me with a social worker to talk about what life would be like for me when I left the hospital. It was agreed that I would go back to live with my mother, and a contract was drawn up about what the rules would be.

My parents and I would have heated arguments about what school I would go to and about my being gay. I told them it wasn't any of their business who I slept with. They disagreed and said I was just confused and that I would grow out of it. They would talk to me about AIDS, trying to scare me into not being gay.

I told them that I already knew a lot about AIDS and ways to prevent getting it. They acted as if I was stupid and didn't know anything. I would tell them about ways you can and cannot get it, and that if I had sex I would always use a condom no matter what the circumstances. I also told them that I was not sexually active, which was true. They acted as if I would get AIDS from the air just because I was gay. They were so ignorant in so many ways.

My mother and I would talk about what my being gay meant to our relationship. I explained to her that I was still the same person and that it didn't matter. My mother would tell me that she was upset because she was not going to have any grandchildren from me. That made me angry. "Who are you thinking about," I asked her, "you or me?"

After two months I left the hospital and went to live with my mother. I decided to go to the Harvey Milk School, a high school for gays, lesbians, and bisexuals, and things have gotten a lot better since then. I have plenty of friends and am happy with my life. Coming out to my family was hard, but now that I have, I can tell my parents almost anything and they give me all the support in the world. I'm also involved in a lot of political causes as well as writing for a teen magazine. And I'm graduating this month and will be going to college next year.

I know now that I didn't really want to die. If I had, I never would have been able to accomplish any of these things. What I really wanted was to live in a world where I wouldn't have to deal with people's prejudices.

I realize now that suicide is no way out. It's a permanent solution to a temporary problem. There's always another solution even when it seems like there isn't. For me, asking for help and coming out were two big steps towards learning to accept myself and not let other people's stereotypical perceptions of gay people put me down.

WHAT WOULD YOU DO IF
I WAS GAY?

Gina Trapani, 17

I   *All the names in this story have been changed.*

remember sitting on the couch next to my Dad watching the news on television when I was about ten years old. There was a report on about the gay and lesbian parade going on in Manhattan. I did not know what it meant to be gay. I asked my father and he told me, "That's when two men or two women love each other like a boy and girl do."

"Why would someone want to do that?" I asked.

Without ever looking at me, he answered, "Well, they can't help it. Gay people are just born like that, like having brown eyes."

"Oh," I said, thinking that it sounded really weird. But then I became worried. What if I turned out be gay? So I said to my Dad, "What would you do if I was gay, Daddy?" He jumped up and looked at me and said, "Why?"

"I was just wondering," I answered, sorry that I had asked at all.

"Well, you would still be my daughter," he said, sitting down again. But for some reason his answer didn't make me feel any better.

A few years later, during my freshman year in high school, I met Jennifer. We became very close, but I knew that the way I felt about her was very different from the way I felt about my other close friends. I was very possessive of Jennifer and didn't want to share her with anyone else. At times I even felt jealous of the guys she liked.

Soon I began to realize that I liked her as more than just a friend. It was very scary for me to think about it, because I'd heard how the girls in school would talk about "lezzies" and the disgusting things they did. It was hard to figure out whether or not I was just confused, or if I really was a l-e-s...Yuck, I couldn't even say the word.

That summer, because of how out of control I felt, because I couldn't handle the feelings I was having, I ended my friendship with Jennifer. I never told her why.

But I still felt that I had to tell someone what was going on. I decided on my friend Linda, because I looked up to her like an older sister. Sitting in her room one day, I sort of hinted around the subject, trying to find out what she thought. I was so afraid that she was going to squeal the minute I brought it up. But she didn't. She looked at me very carefully and intently and waited for me to finish.

Finally I just spit it out: "Linda, what would you think if I, uh, said that I, um, well if I liked, like, another girl?" There was a moment's pause. I was dying of embarrassment, very ashamed of what I had told her, and very afraid of her reaction.

But she said, "No, no, that's not gross at all."

"Really?" I said, hoping that she meant it.

"Yes," she told me. "Do you want to talk?" That day, Linda made me feel much better. She told me that I wasn't bad or disgusting, and that it was okay to feel that way. For me, that talk was the first time I ever outwardly admitted to myself and another person how I felt. (About a year later, I was not so surprised to find out that Linda was a lesbian herself.)

Even though speaking to Linda made me feel better, there were many times when I felt really down and isolated. I didn't know of anyone else in the world who was gay or had even questioned herself. I was afraid to tell anyone in school. I felt very left out because I didn't have a boyfriend, and my friends would always be talking about guys—who they liked, who they were taking to the prom. I didn't belong with them because I wasn't a part of that world and didn't want to be.

Marilyn and Elaine were my two best friends. We had been in school together since first grade. They were always there for me and always understood me when I had a problem. I was sure that after they got used to the idea they would open up to me and everything would be the same as it had always been between us. So I just said straight out, "I think that I am a lesbian."

They were shocked. They asked me a couple of questions. But after that one time, they never mentioned it again. Soon we started to talk less and less about anything at all. I don't know if who I am caused that to happen. But I do know that it made me feel really bad. I learned the hard way that they were not my real friends, and I also learned that I had to be very careful about who I told and who I absolutely could not tell.

It was and still is very frustrating for me to have to live a lie out of fear of other people's reactions. As a result, I began to really appreciate the few people I could tell—all of whom were straight. But I felt like they couldn't really understand, because they hadn't experienced it. Finally I decided that it was time I went out and found people who I could talk to, who would understand how I felt: other gays and lesbians my age.

I remember standing outside the door of a drop-in center for gay teens in Greenwich Village, afraid to go inside. I had no idea what to expect, and I was petrified that I wouldn't fit in there, either.

Finally, I just walked in. A funny-looking girl with a baseball cap on came up to me and said, "Hi, I'm Marie." Marie became one of my best friends—a real best friend, because I know that she loves me for who I am, completely.

A couple of months ago, Marie told me about a group that was forming for lesbian and bisexual women who are under twenty-one. The next week I went to one of their meetings and the women there made me feel right at home. It felt great to be able to goof around with them, joking about ourselves and the people around us. If I talked like that with my straight friends, they wouldn't understand. Ever since that first meeting, I've gone back every week. I've finally found a place where I can be myself and belong.

MY FIRST LOVE:
TOO MUCH, TOO SOON

Anonymous, 17

All the names in this story have been changed.

"Yo, girl, look over there," my friend Terrence told me. "You see that boy? He wants to get with you."

This was back in seventh grade. Terrence had come up to me during fourth period and pointed toward a boy who was standing on the other side of the classroom. He told me the boy's name was Roger. I looked over to where he was pointing and grinned.

It turned out that I already knew who this guy Roger was. He had been staring at me for weeks. I would catch him looking at me in the hallway when we were changing classes and when I was hanging out on the steps talking to my friends. I knew he liked me and I had been wondering when he was going to make his move.

"I told him I knew you ever since you been in my old elementary and I would introduce you to him," Terrence said. All I could think was, Oh, how ugly this person is. Roger's face was bumpy and you could see where he scratched his pimple and it burst. And the way he dressed! He had on rundown faded black jeans and sneakers with holes in them and a striped shirt with bleach stains on it.

Terrence and I walked over to where Roger was standing. I said, "Hi, how are you?" and he said, "Hi. Fine. And you?" Afterwards, he did not stop looking at me that whole day. When I caught him, he would smile—he did have a pretty smile—and I would say to myself, "Why is he looking at me?" But I would smile back to be nice and then go on with my schoolwork.

Roger finally approached me during seventh period. I had my head down because I was tired and it was almost the end of the day. When I lifted it up, he was in my face. I gave him a little shy blush. That must have made his day because he would not stop grinning at me. He asked me how I was. I told him fine. Then I asked him, "Why are you still grinning at me?" He told me, "I guess it is something about you, I guess."

He asked me if I had a boyfriend. I told him no. Then he asked me for my phone number. I asked him why. "Because I want to call you," he said. I said, "Well...I don't know," but I gave it to him. Despite his appearance, I was starting to like him. I thought he was very charming.

When we changed to the next class, the teacher assigned Roger and me seats right next to each other. Just before class started I dropped my pen by his chair—not on purpose. We both bent down to pick it up and our heads touched.

As I walked home with my friends after school, I wondered about Roger. Was he really going to call or was it a game? I did my homework and watched TV. Just as I was about to fall asleep, the phone rang. It was Roger. We stayed on the phone for an hour talking about stupid things like each other's ex's. Then I got tired, told him I would talk to him in school the next day, and hung up.

After that, Roger and I started talking several times a day—before school, after school, and then on the phone at least two times almost every night. At school, I continued to catch him staring at me. Before long, his friends were coming up to me to tell me how he felt about me. They would say, "Yo, you know Roger likes you. He just don't know how to say it."

I was thinking, "Oh for real!" I was starting to like Roger a lot. It's true that when I first saw him, I thought he was the ugliest person on the face of the earth. But as I got to know him, I saw that he was also sweet and charming. I started to fall in love with his personality and sense of humor. He used to laugh and joke around and try to cheer me up when I was feeling down.

After about two weeks of talking every day, he told me that he liked me a lot and that was the reason why he couldn't stop looking at me. I was shocked but happy to hear it finally come out of his mouth and not someone else's. But I was still confused about Roger. I just had this feeling that he was after only one thing—sex.

Our relationship went on and off for about a year because I was so confused. But we were spending a lot of time together. We would walk in the park hand in hand, I would go over to his house to spend the day with him, and of course, we continued to talk on the phone. Sometimes I would avoid him for a couple of weeks, but we would always get back together. I felt like I could not get enough of him. Whenever I was bored I would go see him. I was beginning to think I loved him.

One night, after we had known each other for about a year, Roger called me and asked me if I had ever had sex. I said, "No, why?" He had asked me once before, back in seventh grade. That time we had been sitting in class and I had just acted like I didn't hear what he said. He let it go and we went on with our conversation. This time was different. Roger said, "Since we have been together for a year and you have made me wait, when are we going to do it?"

I was so scared. I did not know what to say. I thought, "Oh my God, not me!" I asked him when he wanted to do it and he said, "Whenever you feel like it. It's your decision." I thought maybe it would be good to just get it over with, not to have to talk about it anymore. So I said, "What about Wednesday after school?" But I was thinking, "Do I really want to do this? Am I making the right decision or am I rushing into it?"

After I got off the phone I was up all night thinking about whether I should do it or wait. Part of me thought I was ready. I knew that I was falling in love with Roger and it was getting boring, just having a talk-and-visit relationship. But I wasn't sure. I cried when I thought about all the things that could go wrong. What if we did it and something stupid happened, like me getting pregnant or him just getting up and leaving?

Wednesday came and the day went by so fast. It was like the hours were rushing by because they knew what was waiting for me after school. I told my best friend Rochelle and she could not believe it—she kept on asking me if I was scared. Of course I was! Every time I saw Roger he was looking at me and grinning. Whenever I walked by him, he would pull my arm and whisper in my ear to wait for him after school. "Don't leave," he'd say.

The next thing I knew, the day was over. The moment I stepped off the front steps onto the sidewalk, Roger called to me. "Wait," he said, "Where are you going?" I told him, "Nowhere. I'm waiting for you." I was playing bad, like I knew what I was doing, but deep down inside I was terrified.

Rochelle and Roger and his friend and I started walking toward Roger's house. Rochelle kept on asking me if I was scared. When we got to Roger's, I begged her to stay for a while, but she couldn't. At one point I was right on her heels, but then I decided to go through with it. Then Roger's friend left and it was only us two in front of the house. I started to wish that it would just happen and be over.

Finally, Roger said, "Let's go inside." He opened the door, I took off my coat and my book bag, and we went downstairs to his bedroom. He locked the door behind us and there was no way out. I decided to go along with the program.

Roger and I sat on his bed and started talking. That led into kissing. The next thing I knew, my shirt came off. Then it happened. I was in so much pain but all I could think about was that I wasn't a virgin anymore.

After it happened I could not look Roger in the face. I was embarrassed that he had seen my body. Nobody before had ever seen my body but my mother. To make me feel better, he lifted up my face and we kissed for a minute or two.

I started to get dressed and we kissed every time I put on a piece of my clothes. Then he walked me halfway home. On the way he bought me Chinese food, but I was not so hungry. All I knew was that I was very sore. When I got home, I took a shower and fell asleep.

After that, sex became a tremendous part of our relationship. I was scared he only wanted one thing, but that didn't stop me from doing it. We started having sex every other day. It was like we were sex fiends—we were so into it. It was like I was a pro after the first time. Every time we were alone we always wound up doing something.

I felt safe and comfortable with Roger. And I felt that since we were having sex, he was only mine and no one else's. That's what went through my mind every time we did it.

I did not give any thought to birth control—all I thought of was being with Roger. Not long after we started having sex, I started to think I was pregnant. Maybe it was because I was nervous about having sex. I told Roger and he did not find it funny. He told me that if I was lying he was not going to speak to me for a long time. He asked me questions like, "What about school?" and "Are you keeping it?" I told him I didn't know. I was real scared.

Then I went to the clinic and found out that I wasn't pregnant after all. That made me happy. They asked if I used birth control. I told them no and looked stupid. They gave me a lot of condoms so I'd have some protection in the future.

Roger and I slowed down some and we also started using the condoms. But after the pregnancy scare, our relationship started to change. We didn't talk as much and Roger started to act like he was bored and wanted to move on. He stopped calling me and after a while we stopped seeing each other. Part of me assumed it was over between us, but another part was still hoping that he would call me to apologize.

Then one day I came into school around third period. The bell to change classes rang as soon as I got into the building. I hit the third floor and everyone was saying "Hi" to me. As I walked up the hall to hug one of my girlfriends, I saw Roger. He was hugging on this girl. I mean hugging all up on her. The worst part was, I knew the girl. Her name was Gail and we had known each other ever since third grade.

I acted like I didn't see them but I knew he had seen me. The same stupid grin he gave me when I first met him was on his face when I saw him wrapped around her. I felt like killing him and I was just as mad at the girl. I thought, "How can Gail do this to me? She knew Roger and I were messing around with each other." And later that day, that jerk Roger had the nerve to ask me, "You ain't my girl no more?" Did he think I would have forgotten what I had seen so quick?

When I got home after school, I cried and told myself to forget about Roger. I did not speak to him for months after that. I could not approach him because my feelings were so hurt. I would cry every night and relive old memories. I felt like I was used for only one thing. I felt betrayed. But even though I was upset with Roger, I still liked him. That's why it hurt so much.

It's been three years since my relationship with Roger ended. I still see him around sometimes, but it is just a hi-and-bye situation. Even so, my feelings for him are still having an influence on my life. Other relationships I have had since Roger do not last long. I always compare the guy to him or talk about him too much or I break up with the new guy because I'm still thinking about Roger. I can't help thinking that we still have something and that our relationship is not over yet.

I feel that a part of me is gone and not coming back. I think if I still had my virginity I would feel better than I do now and that it would be easier for me to start another relationship if any new guy came along. At the time, I didn't think I was rushing into anything because Roger and I had known each other a year before we had sex. But now I realize that I wasn't ready and I should have waited.

V.

Becoming Who I Am

ESSAYS ABOUT CHOICES

BECOMING A VEGETARIAN: A MATTER OF TASTE

Victoria Law, 18

For as long as I can remember, I never really liked the taste of meat. If I ate in a restaurant I would try to order a dish without it. At home, I would feed most of it to my dog under the table.

My father finally got tired of hearing me grumble about having to eat meat and of yelling at me for feeding it to the dog. When I was twelve, he suggested that I become a vegetarian. Since he's a health nut, he pointed out that I had to balance my diet by eating more tofu and soybeans to make up for the lost protein. That wasn't a problem since I liked both. My mother wasn't thrilled but she thought it was a phase I would soon get over.

Although I chose not to eat meat because I couldn't stand the taste, after I made my decision I also started thinking about the ethical reasons for being a vegetarian. I began paying attention to mail from animal rights organizations instead of throwing it out, unopened. After reading their pamphlets about the gruesome way that animals are raised and slaughtered, I felt it was morally wrong to kill animals for food and that I had made the right decision.

At first, I thought it would be really difficult to adjust to not eating meat or poultry. Even though I hadn't liked it, I'd grown up with meat on the table every night. But even though it seemed as if it would be difficult, I was determined to stick by my decision to become a vegetarian.

I did decide to keep seafood in my diet because I felt that I needed something to eat if I went to a restaurant. I didn't want to be stuck having to eat salad every time we went out since I don't like salad very much. Besides, I didn't see anything morally wrong with eating fish since they aren't raised in inhumane conditions and violently slaughtered like livestock and poultry are.

I soon realized that I wouldn't have any trouble sticking to my new diet. I often went to Chinese restaurants with my family and I always found something that suited my taste, like tofu or vegetable dishes. At other restaurants, I simply ordered seafood.

When some of my teachers noticed that I had stopped eating meat, they would tell me that it was unhealthy and that that was the reason I was so skinny. They predicted that I would soon change my mind about my new diet.

A few months after I'd become a vegetarian, the school nurse found out and lectured me about it, trying to change my mind. She thought vegetarianism was unhealthy and that I was destroying my body by depriving it of meat.

Some of my classmates thought that all vegetarians were radical animal rights activists and told me that I wasn't saving animals by not eating meat—the meat industry would go on whether or not I supported it. They couldn't believe I chose not to eat meat because I couldn't stand the taste of it, since most of them lived off of McDonald's and other fast food. Sometimes they would wave a hamburger or a hot dog in front of my face, saying, "Mmmm, meat!" Or they would see me eating a bowl of rice and soybeans or vegetables from home and say something like, "That's not a real meal. No meat!" That really annoyed me because I felt that they were making fun of my decision.

I couldn't understand why they made such a big deal about it. I never waved my food in front of their faces or lectured them about how horrible meat was. Why couldn't people just accept my choice? Instead they made me feel ashamed and I started to wonder if there was something wrong with me.

That changed when I turned fifteen. I met Dave, another teenage vegetarian, at a friend's party. My friend had ordered pizza, and both Dave and I told him to order a pie without pepperoni because we didn't eat meat. He was the first person who didn't make me feel apologetic about my eating habits. Dave was much more radical than I was: he didn't eat red meat, poultry, or fish. He told me that he had tried to eat fish once after becoming a vegetarian and got sick from it. He was also an animal rights activist, boycotting products tested on animals and hassling fur wearers.

After Dave and I started dating, I began to learn and care more about animal rights. I wrote letters to companies that did testing on animals and even started harassing fur wearers. (I've stopped writing letters but still make the occasional remark to the socialite in mink on the street.) Although I didn't stop eating fish altogether, I cut down on it. The fact that Dave didn't eat it made me feel guilty, even though he never said anything.

About six months later I met friends of my aunt and uncle who are Taoists and believe that it is wrong to take any kind of animal life. They are strict vegetarians who don't eat meat, poultry, fish, or even dairy products, because they don't believe in eating anything that comes from an animal. They believe in reincarnation and feel they could be eating their ancestors if they ate meat or fish.

I went to their holy house (a place where they went every Sunday to worship and to learn more about their religion) and soon after my first visit, I stopped eating fish. I realized that I didn't need fish after seeing that the people there could survive without it. Besides, I had started to feel guilty about eating anything that had once had a heartbeat.

My mother and other relatives weren't thrilled about my growing commitment to vegetarianism. When I visited relatives in Canada last Christmas, my uncle, who's a doctor, lectured me about how unhealthy not eating meat was for a growing girl and fed me vitamin pills. My aunt grumbled about how she had to cook me "special dishes." My cousins pointed out that I had eaten fish over the summer and asked why I had suddenly stopped. I told them that I had been influenced by a visit to a Taoist holy house. My mother said that I was just being difficult.

My aunt and uncle in New York aren't any better. My uncle, who hates chicken, tries to get me to eat meat by saying he'll eat chicken if I eat meat. When we go out, they order three or four meatless dishes and when I don't finish all of them, they say they ordered them "just for me." They don't realize that I can't eat every dish they put in front of me, even if it has no meat.

This year I've met a few more vegetarians, so I don't feel so alone. At the library where I work, I found out that one of the younger librarians is also a vegetarian and she and I have talked about the way some people react when they find out. (One of our other co-workers asked us, "You're vegetarians?" in the same tone he would probably use to ask, "You eat insects?") One of the college counselors at school has encouraged me, giving me recipes and even samples of her cooking to get me into vegetarian cooking. What a change from my elementary school nurse!

I don't think I can ever go back and start eating meat again. I can't even stand eating the meat substitutes that some vegetarian restaurants serve because they taste so much like meat. I've tried them and immediately felt like throwing up. I don't plan on becoming a vegan (someone who eats neither meat nor dairy products) either: I like pizza and cheese too much to give them up. I'm more comfortable about my diet now and don't feel defensive when people ask me about it. I simply explain that I don't like the taste of meat and leave it at that. Sometimes I'll expand on it and tell them that ethics also play a part in my decision but aren't the major reason. I know now that most people won't make fun of my choice and a lot of times are interested in it and curious to know more.

A DESIGNER ADDICTION

Delia Cleveland, 21

*M*y name is Dee, and I am a recovering junkie. I was hooked on the strong stuff. Ralph Lauren wore my pockets thin. Calvin Klein was no friend of mine. And then Guess? what—I finally got the monkey off my back, although it took me a while to get on the right track.

I got hooked on Brand Names six years ago when a Polo pusher by the name of Ralph got me to join his posse. It was really easy. If you didn't have a job you could steal to be down with him. I had a part-time job and wasn't making much, but I didn't care. I scraped my last dollar to be able to wear Ralph's emblem on my chest like a badge of honor and respect.

My mother told me I was messing up. Homework didn't matter anymore. Old friends were out. I was too fly to hang with them. Ralph offered me clout. The fellows adored me; the females were jealous. I became a fiend for the attention.

It was all about me and Ralph L. until along came Calvin K., Georges M., and this new guy named Tommy H. Since I was all of that, I had to be down with them too. We exchanged goods: my money for their names.

My mom started nagging me again. Out of worry she started snooping around my bedroom to see where my paycheck was going. She had set up a savings account for me, and I withdrew all of the money—$1,000—to satisfy my habit. Then I charged $600 to my credit card for a quick fashion fix. Things were getting out of hand.

I didn't think I had a problem until the day my mother found the receipt in a shopping bag. She yelled that I was crazy. She wanted to know why I was giving all of my money to men who already had plenty. I told her she was behind the times and didn't know any better. I was looking good, and that's all that mattered...

Until my money started getting tight. I was so busy buying more stuff that I couldn't do anything else. I even resorted to borrowing money from my mother. The more I took from her, the more she rubbed it in—I was sick. I needed help.

Just to prove my mother wrong, I sought help. I wanted to show her that I could stop Brand Names from running my life, any time I wanted. It was my choice.

So, I chose to watch how other Brand Names users lived to see where they were headed. The big shock was, they weren't going anywhere. For example, one guy dipped in Guess? was trying to talk to me in the train station. When the train came in, he asked me if there were any cops on the platform. I shrugged my shoulders and he hopped the turnstile. The guy had on $70 jeans and couldn't afford a token?

A popular jock at my school named Timmy (not his real name) used to boost Ralph Lauren clothing every single weekend. Even after getting locked up, he continued to boost. I got bold and asked him his purpose. "I am taking from the white man," he answered with a sly grin. "Ralph Lauren said his clothes ain't made for black people, so I'm going to keep geeing until I get caught again."

"Get caught?" I wanted to say. "Get handcuffed for 'the white man'?" But I kept quiet, because he—like me—didn't know any better. Timmy couldn't understand that while he was doing jail time for boosting, Ralph Lauren would be collecting cars, furniture, and houses. Would Timmy care that while he was earning zero dollars a year, looking good, Ralph Lauren would still be worth $700 million?

Armed with this new knowledge, I vowed to leave Brand Names alone. I kept the clothes I had and started buying sensible clothes that looked fly. There was plenty to choose from. On the road to recovery, I bought $30 Levi's instead of $70 Guess? jeans. As a reward, with the money saved, I would treat myself to a Broadway play or a funky art museum. That made the withdrawal period less painful. My bank account got fatter and I got stronger.

When my friends started getting heavy into Brand Names, I tried to warn them. But they thought I was jealous and couldn't afford the stuff anymore. I explained that it was my choice not to support the luxury lifestyles of Brand Names dealers. They told me to mind my business; they could afford to wear what they wanted to wear.

I knew they couldn't afford to become dependent on Brand Names. But I couldn't get through to them. Brand Names made them feel like I had once felt—important.

To this day, I see teenagers denying their addiction to Brand Names, even when the warning signs are obvious. If you or some-one you love is going on four-hour bus trips just to get Brand Names; if you're selling drugs, stealing, or spending hard earned money just to get Brand Names, get help.

If you are not using, don't start. Be proud that you can survive without losing your identity to a name other than your own.

People who use Brand Names don't think there's anything wrong with wearing a jacket inside-out to show off a tag. They dress to impress and hang on the corners nodding off to their own Brand Names beat. There's a world of positive buzz, but Brand Names users aren't trying to hear it. The unnatural high keeps users in a lifeless mode—basement parties, the streets…

Brand Names is a powerful addiction that has destroyed many young lives. I was lucky. One outrageous receipt and an angry mother saved me from a life of make believe self-importance. From now on, my money is going to stay in my name. A nickel bag—$500—remains in my checking account. My savings account grows fatter with interest. I entertain myself with the finer things in life. I no longer look the part because I'm too busy living it. Calvin Klein was never a friend of mine. By the way, have you met him yet?

A Rap Fan's Alternative

Allen Francis, 19

Part 1. Finding Nirvana

While I was growing up, the only music anyone ever listened to in my house was rap and r&b. I shunned rock. It was alien to me.

That started to change when I was sixteen. I was watching TV and Nirvana's video "Smells Like Teen Spirit" came on. I remember the thunderous guitar riffs and bass lines. I remember the lead singer's voice, which reminded me of a banshee's wail. I didn't understand a word he was saying, but I didn't give a damn. "I like a rock song," I said to myself. These words are not usually uttered by a hardcore rap fanatic.

I didn't tell anyone in the house that I was starting to like rock. I would have felt like I was turning my back on an old friend. Think about when you were younger and you had one best friend in the world. Then you got older and made more friends and didn't have as much time for your best friend. That's how crossing over musically made me feel. How could I betray my best friend? How could I leave rap?

Meanwhile, I was hearing more mention in the media about Nirvana and their style of music. It seemed like this sound was getting big and part of me wanted to be involved with it. But another part of me felt that there wasn't room in my musical taste for headbanger vomit noise. How could I be devoted to rap and grunge at the same time?

I started to get my answer while watching *Video Music Box's Alternative Thursdays* one day. They played rap that was different from your run of the mill LL Cool J or EPMD. You know, guys like Me Phi Me and P. M. Dawn, whose raps didn't always rhyme and whose videos included weird imagery like puppets onstage or synchronized swimming.

Nirvana's "Come as You Are" came on. I was shocked. I didn't remember the Box playing rock before. And I liked it. The bass line was enchanting, and lead singer Kurt Cobain's voice was hypnotizing. There are some songs where you can press the stop button in the middle without a care, but others you have to hear all the way through. This was one of the others. I couldn't stop listening.

Gradually I came to a realization. If *Video Music Box* could make room for both rock and rap, so could I. My musical taste had room the size of a warehouse; I had just never bothered to fill it.

So I admitted it to myself. I loved Nirvana. If I heard one of their songs on the radio, it got my complete attention. I still didn't tell anyone in my house, or at school. What would they think? I could imagine it now. "I love Nirvana!" They all would take off their rap-blasting headphones, stop reciting their favorite rap lyrics, and stare at me with accusing eyes.

Support came in the form of my English teacher, Mr. Eiferman. He was a kind of hippie from the sixties and would sometimes talk about the latest in rock. Once he brought in a VCR and showed us an *Unplugged* show that featured some rap artists. Then he started to rewind the tape so he could show us the most popular group of that year—Nirvana. Everyone else in the class was less than enthusiastic, but I couldn't wait. Then the bell rang. I was horrified.

The next day I asked Mr. Eiferman if he could make me a tape of Nirvana's latest album. (I didn't even know the name of it.) He agreed and offered to include their first album, *Bleach*. I said no. I was taking this musical transition slowly. I was only interested in the current album. He brought me the tape the next day. I couldn't wait to get home and listen to it.

As soon as I got in the door I headed straight for the tape deck. Then I paused. I wasn't the only one who lived in the house. What would everyone else say? So I closed the door and played it at a low volume. I heard the opening guitar riff to "Teen Spirit" and then braced myself for the bass and the beat. I felt like swinging my head violently back and forth.

After the first song I stopped the tape and rewound it, afraid of what else Nirvana had in store for me. Then I realized I couldn't be afraid anymore to show people I loved the music. My mother was out shopping and only my brothers and sisters were in the house. They were never afraid to blast the music they loved. I turned the volume up and braced myself again—this time for my family's reaction.

The music blasted. No one opened the door. I felt tense, waiting for something to happen. Then the door opened. My brothers Aaron and Austin peered in, looked at me, looked at the tape deck, looked at each other, looked at me again, and then slowly closed the door. I didn't feel comfortable.

The next song came on and at first it reminded me of heavy metal. I didn't know if I could get used to this. My youngest brother Alton came in and stood in the doorway. He took a seat and started singing the words. I never saw Alton so interested in music unless it was Michael Jackson or the theme to *Ghostbusters*. Then I started singing. Then we both started to air guitar. I started to relax. I wasn't alone.

Nirvana opened my mind up to other music that wasn't related to rap. My friend Jessica made me a copy of Pearl Jam's *Ten* and I started subscribing to *Rock Video Monthly*, which sends me a VHS tape of ten new alternative videos every month. In addition to my old faves, A Tribe Called Quest, Red Man, and Wu-Tang Clan, I also started listening to Pearl Jam, the Lemonheads, Eve's Plum, and Stone Temple Pilots. I was reborn.

Part 2. Diving into the Pit

In praise of hip-hop, I had worn certain hairstyles and clothes, used the appropriate slang, even written and performed my own raps. After discovering alternative music, I wanted to honor my new love in visible ways. I started wearing plaid shirts, playing air guitar, and swinging my head back and forth like the novice headbanger I was. But there was one thing I had yet to do: jump into the mosh pit.

Moshing is basically a bunch of people in a contained area pushing, hitting, and jumping into each other while listening to loud music. I got my first taste of moshing when I watched the *MTV Music Awards* a couple years ago. Nirvana was performing "Lithium," and people were slamming into each other and a couple of guys climbed up on the stage and jumped into the crowd. At the time, I thought, "Not a chance in hell..."

But people change. I decided I wanted to do it. I felt that to appreciate the music fully, I had to experience how the people in the pit felt when the bodies started slamming.

I thought I'd have my chance over the summer when Biohazard (a hard metal band) was in town, but plans fell through. Then I attended an alternative concert in Central Park in the hopes that a pit would start, but it didn't. A little while later I found out that House of Pain, a rap group that's a favorite of mine, was appearing at Roseland, a club in Manhattan. Special guests: Biohazard and Korn. I was in there.

When the night arrived, I was excited as hell. I was going to see House of Pain and get to mosh. My younger brother Austin and I arrived about an hour before the show was scheduled to start. Empty, Roseland looked huge. It was filling slowly, but a quick head count confirmed that we were the only black people there. This worried us a bit because there were some creepy-looking people in there. One guy had a Charles Manson T-shirt on.

By showtime there was still only a handful of black people in the place, but we relaxed because we came to have a good time, not cause trouble. I started talking to a guy who told me that the pit goes crazy for Biohazard, which almost made me reconsider.

Korn was the opening act, and I wasn't really interested in them because I didn't know who they were. But then I heard them, and they were hype. They played heavy metal and the lead singer had these long dreadlocks that he swung back and forth violently to the music. He was enveloped in a red spotlight, and I couldn't take my eyes off him. Until the pit started.

The pit is usually the area right in front of the stage. I was standing just to the side of it when I noticed that a couple of people had started crowd surfing—holding people aloft and passing them around on a sea of hands. Then I noticed that people had started slamming into each other and that got my full attention. Right around me everyone was calm, but about twenty feet away people were going crazy. With every moment the pit was swelling and getting bigger. If I didn't move, I would soon be swallowed by it.

The pit seemed dangerous. Some people with clenched fists were swinging their arms, not caring who they hit, and I didn't know what I was doing. Then I saw it coming. The pit was coming toward me.

All the calm people rushed away. Then somebody pushed me from behind with his hands, and I pushed the guy I ran into. Then I was pushed and hit from every direction. People fell on me, flailing arms hit me, and I kept getting shoved. My feet were getting caught in other people's legs.

I pushed somebody, my head slammed into another head, and then some guy grabbed me. He hesitated for a second—maybe because I was the only black guy in the pit—and then he pushed me for a couple of feet. I remember getting a little angry, gritting my teeth, and pushing him off me. I had a minute to catch my breath and look at the stage before someone pushed me again.

I started pushing whoever I saw. Korn finished playing and I was still pushing people. It was like a high. I had never experienced anything like it before—violence that didn't get out of hand. It felt good to let off some steam, to express some of the anger inside of me. I was so excited I wanted to run out of the place, call someone and yell, "I finally moshed!"

I found Austin where I left him, off to the side of the crowd. He saw me and said, "You're crazy, Al, I thought you was fighting that guy!" I told him I was on a buzz and asked him what he thought when he saw me mosh. "You're with your peoples," he said. "Crazy."

I was ready to go back into the crowd, but Austin decided to stay in his spot. He didn't want to get involved; watching was enough for him.

The crew was preparing the stage for Biohazard. I remembered that guy telling me that the pit goes wild for them. Meanwhile, I was concentrating on the people who were crowd surfing. It looked like fun, being carried aloft by everyone. I wanted to try it, but I didn't know how to start.

I watched as five guys next to me got ready to lift someone. He pointed to a direction in the crowd and said, "That way." The guys threw him in the air and he crashed through a group of people before hitting the floor. "Why did they throw him?" I wondered. But was I discouraged?

I walked up to the guys and said, "Fellas, can you launch me?" *Newjack* must have been written all over me because one of them said, "Are you sure?" I said, "Yeah." He asked, "In which direction?" and I said, "I don't care." One guy cupped his hands to give me a leg up while the others grabbed me. I had one foot on the ground and used it to give myself a good jump.

I was up. It happened so fast I hardly remember it. I don't remember feeling hands but I know they were holding me up. I remember having this "I can't believe I'm doing this!" feeling. For about five or six seconds I was crowd surfing. Then, like Nine Inch

Nails, I felt "The Downward Spiral."

My head and torso were going down. I couldn't get a handhold. I was yelling *"Ahhhhh,"* as I landed on my back like the villain in a Bugs Bunny cartoon. One big guy gave me his palm and yanked me off the floor. That was it for me and crowd surfing.

Biohazard started playing and before I knew it I was in the maw of another pit. A forearm hit my upper back. I kept pushing and shoving, but I was losing my breath and I felt a pain in my gut—the kind you feel when you run too fast for too long. I was getting exhausted and if I passed out I would get the living hell stomped out of me. I was trying to get out when I realized there was no way out. The whole ballroom was a pit.

I panicked. What if Austin was in the middle of all this? I pushed and shoved my way out to the border, which was the wall. Austin and everyone who didn't want to mosh were pushed up against the wall. He seemed all right. I think he enjoyed being a neutral witness to the madness.

I joined him and looked back at the pit. It was a blur of people pushing and slamming into each other. Every couple of minutes I'd see two or three people surfing and Biohazard was blasting away. The scene was pure chaos and I loved it, but I'd had my fill.

I'll never forget that night. I'm a very outgoing person, but I don't usually get wild. I don't like hitting people, but it felt good to push and shove the people around me. It was like I was exploding for all the times I kept quiet to avoid an argument or backed down from a fight. For once, I let it all hang out. I doubt if I will do it again anytime soon. But I will do it again.

MOVING INTO THE MAINSTREAM
Slade Anderson, 18

$\mathcal{D}$uring junior high school I went to the New York Institute for Special Education, a school for the blind and visually impaired in the Bronx. It wasn't quite like a regular school. As a blind person I had practically everything I needed: Braille writers, talking computers, Braille books…I was able to run errands for teachers and help other kids get around school and understand their work.

But there were many things about the Institute that I didn't like. A lot of the students had other problems besides being visually impaired or totally blind. Some of them were off in their own worlds and used to talk to themselves, laugh out loud, mimic other people, or jump up and down and rock back and forth. (These weird habits are sometimes referred to as blindisms.)

And that wasn't all. Teachers and staff had to follow you around or know exactly where you were at all times. I hated that. I also hated having to get picked up by a school bus at 6:40 every morning. It was an hour and a half each way between my house in Brooklyn and the Institute, so there was no way I could hang out after school. And if I wanted to go around my own neighborhood, I had to go with my father, mother, or sister.

"What kind of teenage life is this?" I thought. I felt like only half a person.

I felt cut off from my friends from elementary school. I'd see some of them at the Lighthouse for the Blind on Saturdays. These were kids with little or no vision who were going to public school and taking mainstream classes.

My friend Billy was going to Edward R. Murrow, a public high school in Brooklyn. "You should come to Murrow, man. It's cool," he said. He talked about the girls there and the resource room where visually limited kids could go to have their work enlarged, put in Braille, or read out loud to them. Billy was making it in the real world and I wanted that for myself.

Another friend of mine, Mike, told me about the Christmas parties they had. It sounded like if I went to that school, I'd have everything I ever wanted: girls, friends, parties, popularity, and people to help me with my print work.

One day after going to the Lighthouse, I approached my mother about it. I told her I wanted to go to Murrow. I told her Billy went there along with other kids who were totally blind. "I want to broaden my social life," I said. "And my grades are good so I know I can do well in a mainstream class." The next day we took a bus ride just to see how far Murrow was from my house.

After that, I made an appointment to visit the school. When I got there, there were a million kids in the hallway. I went upstairs and met Mrs. Simon, the resource room teacher, and saw some of my old friends. Mrs. Simon asked my friend Chris to show me around. I'd never seen such a big school all in one building or met so many nice people. "You get around this big school without getting lost?" I asked Chris.

He just laughed and said, "You'll get it down in no time."

In one of the hallways I met a kid named Ricky who was totally blind. He had a guide dog and a lot of girls around him. "Just imagine that being me," I thought.

For the first week or so, my mother brought me to school. Then I started taking a school bus. Because I already knew so many people, had a resource room where I could get extra help, and was taking special ed. classes at first, the change from the

Institute to Murrow wasn't too drastic.

In the resource room I had people dictate class notes, math problems, or whatever else I couldn't read on my own. The teachers assigned kids to take me from class to class, and if a kid couldn't take me, a teacher or a paraprofessional would do it.

My friend Chris helped me get acclimated to the school. My first year we were in the school production of *The King and I* together. Chris (who has a little vision) helped me get around the stage and interact with the rest of the cast. Chris was very sociable, and knowing there was another person with limited vision getting along with the rest of the kids helped bring me out of my shell. It turned out to be a great experience.

As time progressed I started to take mainstream classes. The first one I remember setting foot into was Spanish. I had taken a little Spanish at the Institute and wanted to see how I'd do, so Mrs. Simon asked the teacher to let me sit in on the class. It moved at a much faster pace than the special ed. classes I was taking. The kids didn't stop the teacher quite as often either. They also behaved a little better.

The teacher gave us a list of new words. She'd say the word and then the whole class would repeat it. I could pretty much follow that. But when she started to give out handouts I really felt isolated. I took the handouts anyway and went over them later with someone in my resource room. A lot of the low vision kids had to do that or ask one of the kids next to them for help.

While I was working toward becoming mainstreamed, I also took mobility training. We made a tactual map (a raised map you can feel with your fingertips) of the school and I learned how the hallways and classrooms were set up numerically. I also found my way around using landmarks like cracks on the floor, pillars, and garbage cans.

I worked on the bus trip to and from the school with Cindy, my mobility teacher. We practiced getting to the bus stop, then taking the bus home, and finally making the trip to school. It took a lot of work but on the morning that she told me I was finally "cleared" to travel by myself, it was almost like getting a license to drive. That's how free I felt. It was a big accomplishment.

But mainstreaming isn't something that happens overnight and then you're done. You have to work at it. The bus I had to take didn't run very often and sometimes it would rush right past me without stopping. After a while I made friends with some of the drivers, though, and they would know to stop for me. One driver knew me so well that when I wasn't on his bus in the morning, the next day he'd ask me, "Playing hooky again, huh?"

Even after I worked my way out of special ed. and was taking regular classes with sighted kids, I still had obstacles to overcome. During one cycle I had gym class on the fourth floor. To get there you had to go through two different gyms and up a flight of stairs. After I changed out of my gym clothes I never had enough time to get to math class. The teacher told me he didn't mind my being late, but I felt uncomfortable about it. It made me appear disabled.

Without consulting my resource room teacher I went straight to my guidance counselor and requested a schedule change. When Mrs. Simon heard about it she was upset. She felt I was going over her head—and getting in over mine. She said the class I had requested had a teacher who once had a bad experience with a blind student and she was concerned about that. I took the class anyway and got an "excellent."

With every success story there is a little hardship, however. People still shy away from me because I'm visually impaired. Sometimes instead of saying "Hi, Slade" they say, "Watch that stick." Others feel embarrassed if I ask them to read something to me softly.

Going into a mainstream program was a big and scary decision, but I'm still glad I made it. Life at the Institute was too sheltered. At Murrow I learned that I can't always have a Braille book handed to me at the same time the print users get theirs. I learned that there is life outside the blind world and if I want to be a part of it, I have to go out and take some risks.

CLIMBING THE GOLDEN ARCHES

Marissa Nuñez, 19

*T*wo years ago, while my cousin Susie and I were doing our Christmas shopping on Fourteenth Street, we decided to have lunch at McDonald's.

"Yo, check it out," Susie said. "They're hiring. Let's give it a try." I looked at her and said, "Are you serious?" She gave me this look that made it clear that she was.

After we ate our food, I went over to the counter and asked the manager for two applications. I took them back to our table and we filled them out. When we finished, we handed them in to the manager and he told us he'd be calling.

When Susie and I got home from school one day about a month later, my mother told us that McDonald's had called. They wanted to interview us both. We walked straight over there. They asked us why we wanted to work at McDonald's and how we felt about specific tasks, like cleaning the bathrooms. Then they told us to wait for a while. Finally the manager came out and said we had the job.

When we got outside, I looked over at Susie and laughed because I hadn't thought it would work. But I was happy to have a job. I would be able to buy my own stuff and I wouldn't have to ask my mother for money anymore.

A week and a half later we went to pick up our uniforms (a blue and white striped shirt with blue pants or a blue skirt) and to find out what days we'd be working. We were also told the rules and regulations of the work place. "No stealing" was at the top of the list. A couple of the others were: "Leave all your problems at home" and "Respect everyone you work with."

Before you can officially start working, you have to get trained on every station. I started on "fried products," which are the chicken nuggets, chicken sandwiches, and Filet-o-Fish. Then I learned to work the grill, which is where we cook the burgers. Next was the assembly table where we put all the condiments (pickles, onions, lettuce, etc.) on the sandwiches. After all that, you have to learn the french fry station. Then finally you can learn to work the register. It was a month before I could be left alone at any station.

The most difficult thing was learning how to work the grill area. We use a grill called a clamshell which has a cover. It cooks the whole burger in forty-four seconds without having to flip it over. At first I didn't like doing this. Either I wouldn't lay the meat down right on the grill and it wouldn't cook all the way through or I would get burned. It took a few weeks of practicing before I got the hang of it. Now, after a lot more practice, I can do it with no problem.

My first real day at work was a lot of fun. The store had been closed for remodeling and it was the grand opening. A lot of people were outside waiting for the store to open. I walked around just to get the feel of things before we let the customers come in. I was working a register all by myself. My cousin was at the station next to me and we raced to see who could get the most customers and who could fill the orders in fifty-nine seconds. I really enjoyed myself.

Susie worked for only three months after our grand opening, but I stayed on. I liked having a job because I was learning how to be a responsible person. I was meeting all kinds of people and learning a lot about them. I started making friends with my co-workers and getting to know many of the customers on a first-name basis. And I was in charge of my own money for the first time. I didn't have to go asking Mom for money when I wanted something anymore. I could just go and buy it.

Working at McDonald's does have its down side. The worst thing about the job is that the customers can be real jerks sometimes. They just don't seem to understand the pressure we're under. At times they will try to jerk you or make you look stupid. Or they will blame you for a mistake they made. If you don't watch and listen carefully, some of them will try to short-change you for some money.

The most obnoxious customer I ever had came in one day when it was really busy. She started saying that one of my co-workers had overcharged her. I knew that wasn't the case, so I asked her what the problem was. She told me to mind my own business, so I told her that she was my business. She started calling me a "Spanish b-tch" and kept on calling me names until I walked away to get the manager. If I had said anything back to her, I would have gotten in trouble.

Another time, a woman wanted to pay for a $2.99 Value Meal with a $100 bill. No problem, we changed it. She walked away from the counter with her food and then came back a few minutes later saying we had given her a counterfeit $20 bill in her change. We knew it was a lie. She wouldn't back down and even started yelling at the manager. He decided that we should call the cops and get them to settle it. That got her so mad that she threw her tray over the counter at us. Then she left. Of course, not all our customers are like this. Some are very nice and even take the time to tell the manager good things about me.

Sometimes we make up special events to make the job more fun for everyone. For example, we'll have what we call a "battle of the sexes." On those days, the women will work the grill area and the french fry station and all the other kitchen jobs and the men will work the registers. For some reason, the guys usually like to hide in the grill area. The only time they'll come up front and pretend they are working there is to see some female customer they are interested in. Still, they always act like working the grill is so much harder than working the register. I say the grill is no problem compared to working face-to-face with customers all day. After a battle of the sexes, the guys start to give the girls more respect because they see how much pressure we're under.

Every six months, our job performance is reviewed. If you get a good review, you get a raise and sometimes a promotion. After my first six months on the job I got a raise and was made a crew trainer. I became the one who would show new employees how to work the register, fry station, and yes, even the grill area.

When I made a year and half, I was asked if I would like to become a manager-trainee. To move to that level, your performance has to be one hundred percent on all stations of the store. That means doing every job by the book with no shortcuts. The managers have to trust you, and you have to set a good example for your co-workers. I was so happy. Of course I said yes.

Now that I've been there two years, the managers trust me to run a shift by myself. I am working to get certified as a manager myself. To do that I have to attend a class and take an exam, and my manager and supervisor have to observe the way I work with everyone else and grade my performance. I have been in the program for nine months now and expect to get certified this month. I'm thinking about staying on full-time after I graduate from high school.

Working at McDonald's has taught me a lot. The most important thing I've learned is that you have to start at the bottom and work your way up. I've learned to take this seriously—if you're going to run a business, you need to know how to do all the other jobs. I also have more patience than ever and have learned how to control my emotions. I've learned to get along with all different kinds of people. I'd like to have my own business someday, and working at McDonald's is what showed me I could do that.

GROWING INTO FATHERHOOD

Julio Pagan, 18

Starting when I was about twelve, I began thinking about having a son, someone I could play with and teach my strange and crazy philosophy.

I was always good with my little cousins and nephews. I would play with them, and they'd laugh. I would read them stories I'd written and take them to the park so they could learn how to play football. It felt good having them around, and I knew I wanted a child of my own some day. But I never expected to have one at such an early age.

I was sixteen and a junior in high school when I met Maria (not her real name). She was fifteen and a freshman. I was playing the drums for a band in church and she would send me little notes with my sister. I thought this was childish, but I liked it.

We started going out. Sometimes, she would sleep over at my house after attending night services at our church in Manhattan because it was too late for her to travel back to Brooklyn alone. She usually bunked with my sister.

One night, about a month into our relationship, Maria stayed over on a really hot night. I had a fan in my room and my sister didn't. It was about two o'clock in the morning when Maria walked into my room to ask if I would lend her the fan. I asked why, when all she had to do was sleep in my room. After thirty minutes of persuasion, she agreed. And that night it happened—we made love.

Two months later, during the month of May, she told me she was pregnant! Other girls have told me that just to get my reaction, so at first I thought she was playing around. Then I noticed her eyes were watery and that she had this serious look on her face. When I finally came to my senses, I began to think: what about school, what about my job, what about me?

Actually, I was not as worried about her being pregnant as I was about telling my parents. My father had his first child when he was seventeen and always warned me not to make the same mistake. He explained to me that having a child when you're young causes problems, like having to get a job and having to drop out of school.

The same thing happened to my cousin, who had his first child when he was in his senior year in high school and never graduated. After that he had six other children and he never got a G.E.D. or went to college. My father told me that if it happened to me, I would have to face it on my own.

An abortion was out of the question because I didn't have much money and I didn't know about places that offered free services. When I told Maria, she started to cry as if her life was over. I admit I really thought mine was too. But we talked and came to a decision.

She would have the baby and I would help her in any way I could. While she was pregnant I would travel to Brooklyn every other day to visit her. After the baby was born, I would take care of him during the week so she could go to school and she would have him on the weekends.

We did it that way because I was closer to graduation and I knew I would find a way to finish. I didn't want to be responsible for Maria messing up her life the way my cousin did. After she graduated, she would take the baby during the week and I would be the one to see him only on weekends.

After a couple of days, we talked all this over with our parents. Our mothers were surprised but not angry. But when my father found out, all hell broke loose. He told me that I would not be able to stay in the house any longer. He explained how the trust he had for me was gone and how it would take a long time for it to be regained.

During the months Maria was pregnant, our relationship got a little rocky. We would argue almost all the time. I would tell her not to smoke but she would anyway. Or we would argue for no reason at all. We started seeing and talking to each other less and less every month. I think our relationship just wore out. It got to the point where she didn't even want me around her.

Even though we weren't together, I still wanted her to have the child. My feelings for the baby didn't change, I guess, and neither did my feelings for Maria.

The night she went into labor, we were in church. It was about 9:00 p.m. and my parents rushed her to Lincoln Hospital in the Bronx.

That night was the most paranoid night of my life. All the feelings I held inside since the day she told me exploded. I used the bathroom at least five times. All sorts of things went through my mind. Is it going to be a boy or a girl? Is it going to be deformed? And a question I didn't enjoy asking myself: Is my child going to die? I was worried about that because my grandmother's first child died shortly after its birth.

I always saw myself as a strong person, but this was too much to handle. I didn't go into the delivery room simply because I couldn't. Maria had been angry at me the whole time and I guess I couldn't handle all that pressure. Her mother went in instead of me.

By 2:00 a.m., I was very tired but couldn't fall asleep with all the things going through my mind. Finally, the doctor came into the waiting room. He told us there were some difficulties and my heart just hit the floor. He then explained it was common with young mothers and they just had to perform a simple operation.

The first time I saw the baby, it didn't feel like he was mine. It felt just like the times when I used to go to the hospital to see my cousin's children. I didn't feel like a father.

It's been a year and a couple of months now since Israel's birth (it was my mother's idea to give him a biblical name). Maria kept the baby with her for the first five months to establish a motherly relationship. She knew she wasn't going to see him much after he came to live with me.

I've moved out of my parents' house (my father wasn't kidding about my having to deal with this on my own), and during the week Israel stays with me. Most of the time my grandmother takes care of him while I'm at work or school. There are times when Maria comes over to stay for a while when she has a fight with her parents, but that doesn't happen too often.

I usually spend about two hours with Israel in the morning and five more when I come home from work. When I get home he is usually in his stroller raising hell with my grandmother. I quickly take him out before he starts crying (something he always does when I come home to get me to pay attention to him). We'll play with a collection of different balls I've gotten for him or I'll sit him down in front of the window so he can see the kids play outside. I always bring him a bag of Cheese Doodles (his favorite food) and I enjoy watching as he eats them.

At times I feel I don't spend enough time with him, but I can't. I was in my senior year when he was born and I had to work and miss school a lot so I didn't graduate. Now I'm working hard so I can finish this year. I plan to enter college next fall. If I don't sacrifice a couple of hours with him now and finish school, I feel like he isn't going to have a good financial life when he grows up. How would he feel if his father didn't graduate from high school or didn't go to college? What kind of example would I be?

Right now, Maria sees Israel only on the weekends. I don't think he realizes that she's his mother; he thinks my grandmother is. I do admit I won't feel like a true father myself till I'm older. Right now, I'm more like a big brother to him. But I am trying to teach him how to grow up strong and not to take life too seriously all the time.

Since the time Maria and I separated, I've often thought about her moving in with me permanently, but I guess it will take a long time before we can be a real family. I worry about what's going to happen when Israel moves back in with her. I've gotten used to seeing him every day, watching him dance when the radio's on or seeing him drive my grandmother crazy by throwing stuff to her and then running away. I don't ever want to be just a weekend father.

MY ROAD
DOESN'T LEAD TO COLLEGE

Brandy Scelzo, 17

When people ask me what I'm going to do after high school, I tell them that my dream is to drive across the country. I want to drive through every little town, and if I come across something I like, I'll just pull over and stay till I'm bored. When they ask, "What about college?" I tell them that it's not for me, at least not in the near future.

When I was younger I always thought I would go to college. My parents made it sound like just another part of life, something that everyone had to go through. I never really thought twice about it. I just figured that when the time came, I would go.

Another reason I just assumed I'd go to college is that in grammar school and junior high, I always did very well. I never really killed myself studying—it just came easy to me.

But when I got to high school it was a completely different story. In order to keep up in class you had to do the homework, and it usually took hours because there was so much. I tried to find shortcuts and started to hand in incomplete work. Eventually I stopped doing the homework and found myself way behind and very confused.

By the end of my freshman year I had no desire to try to catch up. Having to sit in a class where I didn't know what was going on and knowing that I wasn't going to pass unless I made up forty-six homework assignments made me feel overwhelmed and frustrated. My attendance started to slip.

Once I fell into a routine of failing one class after the next, it was too hard to get out. Now I'm a junior and I'm in my second high school. I still can't seem to make it to school every day even though I know that every time I cut a class I'm limiting my options for the future.

But I also know that if I can't deal with the pressures of high school I won't last two minutes in college. I've been to visit my older sister at her school in upstate New York a few times. All you see on the campus are kids everywhere, a bunch of people who have been let loose for the first time in their lives.

It seems like a lot of fun, but with all that distraction it would be hard for me to keep up with the work. I can't sit at home and do homework if I know that there is something else that I'd rather be doing, which happens to be almost anything.

About a year ago, when I started to do really badly in school, I told my parents I probably wasn't going to college after high school. They didn't think it was a bad decision, but they did want to make sure that if I change my mind some day I'll still have options. They want to make sure that I finish high school at least.

I think my mother especially wants all of her children to go to college. She didn't get to go until she was in her thirties and already had three children and a job. I know it was very hard for her, and she doesn't want that for me.

Other people have told me that I have to go to college and get a job and save my money before I set out on my trip across the country. But I have a problem with that. I've heard so many stories of people having dreams like the ones I have. These people went to college and got jobs. Then they got stuck in routines that were only supposed to be short term but wound up lasting their whole lives. Their original dreams and goals are just something that they wind up telling their kids about. I don't want that to happen to me.

I've never wanted to listen when people tried to tell me all the reasons I can't do what I want to do. They say that there is really no way that I could make it across the country without any money. And I won't have any money if I don't get a good job. And that I can't get a good job if I don't go to college. I'm mad at them for trying to discourage me. I tell them that college isn't for everyone and there are people who don't go to college who live very happy lives. And if I really don't want to go, then why shouldn't I be one of the happy ones?

I'm not interested in having a competitive career like a lawyer or a doctor. My first job was as a cashier in an arts and crafts store, and I liked doing that kind of work just fine. I just want to work in stores and restaurants—the kind of jobs that I would be able to get anywhere in the country I decide to live.

Also, I want the kind of job where, when I'm done for the day, there is no work to take home or worry about. But my parents are scared that I'll never have a way of supporting myself. And as I get older, that worries me too. I now know that even those jobs aren't that easy to get.

One thing that makes the decision to travel easier is that my best friend, Diane, plans to take a year off after high school and go with me. But after that she wants to go to college and I know that she'll have no problem because she's always done pretty well in school. When she's ready to go back to school, I still plan to keep traveling. It will probably be hard for me to be alone at first, but once I get used to it I'm sure I'll be fine.

I don't know what I want to do after I drive across the country. Right now I don't think that I'll ever want to completely settle down anywhere. The worst possible thing that I could imagine is winding up living in a house with a husband and kids and going to work every day. I don't want to be tied down to anything. I want to be able to get up and go whenever I please.

Even though I'm sure now that I don't want to go to college, I'm scared of the possibility that I'll wake up one morning when I'm much older and want to go. By then it might be too late. It frightens me to realize how my goofing off in high school could affect my future.

Despite my fears, I still want to go across country more than anything. I have a feeling that I'll find something, something that I'll love and want to do for the rest of my life. I've been going to school for about eleven years and I haven't found it there, so it's logical that I try going somewhere other than school to find it.

DORM LIFE IS HEAVEN

Donna Hutchinson, 19

*L*ast year, when I applied to Eugene Lang College (a small private school located in Greenwich Village) I didn't ask for on-campus housing because of the cost. Having to pay almost $6,000 a year to live in a dorm was a no-no. I told myself that I could easily commute from my parents' home in Brooklyn.

Over the summer, I had to take some pre-freshman classes. It was an opportunity to familiarize myself with the classrooms, facilities, and workload before officially starting college in September. But more importantly, it was a chance to prove to the school that I could handle college-level work. I had to do well.

My classes went from 9:00 a.m. to 5:00 p.m., Monday through Friday. I usually went to the school's computer center after class to type my papers because I didn't have a typewriter at home. Often I didn't get home until 11:00 p.m. Sometimes I feared having to travel so late all alone. I was usually the only girl in the subway car, surrounded by about ten men. But all my papers had to be handed in typed, double-spaced, and on time—no exceptions and no excuses—so I had no choice.

At least when the program started, I had my own room at home. Then my folks suddenly decided to rent it to a college student. That meant my twenty-three-year-old sister and I would have to share her room.

I told my sister how important it was for me to do well in my classes and asked her to respect my space and use discretion when playing music and talking on the telephone. I had to have quiet time to study. But she continued to play the music as loud as she wanted and to talk on the telephone at all hours of the night.

One day, I left a few piles of assignments I had to complete for class the next day by my bed. When I got home that night—tired and hungry, with my eyes red and the muscles in my neck tense—I found one big pile. I looked at my sister, who was talking on the telephone as usual. "Your junk is messing up my room and I had to arrange it," she said. I looked at her as though I was about to eat her alive. The day before, I had spent at least two hours organizing those papers. Now I had to do it all over again.

That made me so angry. I was trying to get an education, to do something with my life, and my family was making it harder for me. I thought my sister would understand the importance of an education. I had already tried speaking to her nicely about it. Now I wanted to just destroy the outlet in the wall or throw her radio out the window. Everything about her—her face, her voice, her laughter—made me burn with anger.

I didn't argue with her because I didn't have the time or the energy. I took the pile of papers and went to sit in the hallway. I spent another two hours sorting my papers again.

That's when I decided that living in a dorm might be worth the money. If I was going to make it through school, I needed my own space. I talked to a counselor at Lang about moving on-campus. When I received a letter in the mail that said I was getting housing, I was so happy that I cried.

So far, dorm life has been great. My roommate is an international student from Malaysia. We have become good friends and talk about everything: school, boys, people we don't like, celebrities. When I have to study she talks on the phone quietly, and she uses headphones when she plays her music. Sometimes she can get on my nerves—like when she leaves her art supplies all over my side of the room or on the kitchen table. But overall we have a lot in common and get along well.

My dorm is different from most. It's more like an apartment building. I have a kitchen, stove, and refrigerator. Most students cook, or else they eat out. (The school cafeteria is open only on weekdays, and the meal plan is very expensive.) It's just like living on your own. I like being so independent. I come and go as I want. I don't have anyone telling me what to do.

Living in the dorm is convenient too. I can stay in the computer center until closing at 11:00 p.m., and don't have to worry about traveling home late because the dorms are just five blocks away.

When I get home, I'll talk to students who have their doors open. They all say, "Hey, Donna, what's up?" There is always something interesting to talk about and laugh about. Sometimes I invite my friends over to my room. We sit and talk over tea. Other times, I go over to their rooms and check out their collections of books and music. I get to borrow some of them, too. There is always someone around who has something that I don't have (and is willing to lend it), or who knows something that I don't know.

It's a very friendly atmosphere. On Thanksgiving, I found a list of names posted on my friend Mike's door. It said, "Ten things to be thankful for this Thanksgiving." My name was on the list with nine others.

At home, all I heard was my sister cursing at me, saying that she couldn't wait until I got out of *her* room. But in the dorm, I am appreciated, recognized, and treated as somebody who is important.

I am also glad that I stayed here in the city for college instead of going to a town surrounded by bushes where I would have to learn my way around all over again. I have the best of both worlds. My old friends and loved ones are minutes away. But I also have the opportunity to explore the city more than I did when I lived at home.

I had to take out a loan to pay for the dorm, but it's worth it. I don't have to go to the store for my mother, or hear her complain about the dishes in the sink. And I don't have to deal with my sister stressing me. Surprisingly, now that we are away from each other, we have become the best of friends. She calls me at school, and we have friendly conversations. And my mother wants to know when I am coming home to visit. Before she was always busy working; even though we lived in the same house, I sometimes didn't see her for weeks. She never seemed to mind. But now that I am not living with them, my family misses me.

Being away from my family has also made me look at myself in a different light and see my strengths and weaknesses more clearly. I wouldn't be able to do that at home because I'd feel trapped by the memories of our lives together. On my own, I am becoming aware of the world, where I stand in it, and I've started pulling myself up by my bootstraps. It's helping me to be mature, responsible, and grow at a faster rate.

People might think that living in a dorm is not for them because they have a wonderful relationship with their family, their college is in their hometown, and it's far cheaper to commute. I understand that. Many students I know stay at home because of the expense. But for me, the benefits of living on campus outweigh the costs. I'm making new friends in an environment filled with serious-minded people who motivate me.

Some of my old friends and my parents say, "You'll be paying back the government for the rest of your life." Maybe I will be, but at this stage in my life, I am young and energetic, and I want to explore and experience new things. I wouldn't be able to do that in the same way if I were still living at home.

I think every good in life has a price. If I have to pay something in exchange for my growth and development, I am happy to do it.

VI.
Speakout on Writing

SPEAKOUT ON WRITING

*W*e asked six of the young authors whose work is included in this book to share some of their insights into the writing process. On the following pages, Mohamad Bazzi ("My Lebanese Passport"), Zeena Bhattacharya ("Home Is Where the Hurt Is"), Loretta Chan ("Dad's Home Cooking," "Tired of Being a Target"), Anita Chikkatur ("A Shortcut to Independence"), Ferentz Lafargue ("The Crew from the Parking Lot"), and Troy Sean Welcome ("My Father: I Want to Be Everything He's Not," "A Girl Takes Control") discuss what they like and don't like about writing, describe how they developed some of the pieces in this collection, and offer beginning writers some practical advice on how to get their thoughts and experiences on paper.

FIRST EXPERIENCES

When did you discover that you like to write?

ZEENA: It was in freshman English, when I was thirteen, that I discovered writing was more than compositions on "How I spent the summer." I loved the short story writing assignments at school—that was the only homework that could keep me up all night. Soon I started writing short stories and plays on my own. At first, writing was a way for me to escape reality. I could go into my dream world and create characters the way I wanted them to be.

MOHAMAD: My seventh-grade English teacher cajoled me into writing for the school paper. I think my first article was about ozone depletion. But soon enough I was writing about school plays, a winter food drive, and the debate team. By writing for a newspaper, I could ask as many questions as I wanted and take on the challenge of finding answers. Journalism captured my imagination and stimulated my mind.

GETTING INSPIRED

Where do your ideas come from? How do you know when something in your life is worth writing about?

TROY SEAN: When something happens to you that's out of the norm, it's usually worth writing about. I got the idea for "A Girl Takes Control" after a girl who was trying to pick me up started feeding me the same lines I usually fed women when I was trying to pick them up. I was shocked by the way she spoke to me: "You in the all-black, come here!" and "You look mad good." These were the exact things that guys usually said to girls they liked. Being talked to that way was a new experience for me and I thought it couldn't be that common.

ANITA: I write about events in my life if I think they are interesting and if I think that there are other teenagers who have had similar experiences. I also write about things in my life if I think others can learn that it isn't the end of the world if you do something unexpected in your life, anything from changing your hairstyle to getting a new job to becoming a feminist. I also choose to write about experiences that, in some way, changed me or made me realize something about myself.

Sometimes things happen in my life that I don't consider worthy of a story at first, like my decision to get a haircut. As it turned out, I had a lot to say on the subject. I wasn't just writing about the haircut but how to deal with family and friends when they disagree with you or hurt you with their words. By the time I was done writing the story, I realized I was quite happy with my decision to cut my hair even if others did not like it. I also saw that there were humorous parts to it, and looking back at the story and experience, I'm able to laugh at myself.

GETTING PERSONAL

Do you worry about how your family and friends may react when you write about them? How do you cope with writing about your personal experiences?

FERENTZ: I had been worrying about whether I'd be dissing my friends if I wrote what I really thought about them in "The Crew from the Parking Lot." Or that I'd be making a fool of myself. Then I realized that if I really did enjoy those times as much as I said I did, I shouldn't be ashamed to tell about them. I decided to let my ego down and just write.

ZEENA: While writing "Home Is Where the Hurt Is," it was hard to make myself think about things I had suppressed for years. Sometimes I felt like I shouldn't be doing this—after all, they were my parents. And at first I was ashamed to write the parts about when I was being beaten. It made me seem so vulnerable and stupid. The physical act of writing made me feel brave. Still, in the back of my mind I could hear my father threatening to take me back to India or yelling at me about how I was disrespecting my culture. I couldn't imagine what he would do if he read the story, but once I got into it, I knew nothing could stop me.

THE WRITING PROCESS

Is it hard for you to get started on a piece of writing? What makes it hard?

TROY SEAN: The ideas usually come to me faster than the ability to put them in writing. I come up with these great ideas, or so I think, but when it comes to putting them down on paper, things get a little difficult. Sometimes it's hard to find the exact right words to express my ideas.

LORETTA: The hardest thing about writing is getting started. The most discouraging thing is a blank piece of paper or blank computer screen.

I have a system for getting started. First of all, everything must be cleaned. I tell myself that I'm just making sure I won't have any excuses for procrastination later on. The most important area that must be cleaned is my workspace. I like to dispose of anything that is irrelevant to the task I'm about to take on, to get rid of those distractions before sitting down to write. Then I must be surrounded by things that will make my experience as enjoyable as possible without reducing productivity. All the nerdy stuff, of course, like pens, the necessary books (including a dictionary and thesaurus) and my notes. Then the stuff people would normally take a break for: a soda, snacks, eyedrops, Tylenol, trash can, gum. Then I'm ready.

How do you actually begin writing?

LORETTA: I tend to start not at the beginning but in the middle. Sometimes I start without knowing what I'm thinking until I write it all down. Organizing my thoughts inside my head is impossible for a person like me who can't go from one to ten without losing count. I take the information in front of me or the thoughts in my head and type away in whatever order they come out. It doesn't matter where I start as long as I get it all out. When I've run out of thoughts, I go back and move things around. It's much easier to put things in the right order once they materialize on the screen of my word processor. Then I write the introduction and the conclusion when I see what I've written as the body of my text.

TROY SEAN: I go straight to the computer and free-write. That is, I write without any particular structure in mind. This helps me get all my ideas on paper without worrying about the spelling, grammar, or organization. Free-writing is something that everyone can do. It takes no special skill or talent—all you have to do is write.

How do you fell about revising what you've written? When and how do you do it?

FERENTZ: When I handed in my second draft of the parking lot story, I thought I was finished. I sat there with a Kool-Aid smile on my face as my editor read it over, waiting for the instant when he'd enthusiastically exclaim, "This is wonderful. It can go in just like this!"

Dream on, Ferentz. My editor said I had left out the introduction from the first draft and the stuff I had mentioned about playing football and skiing in the winter. He told me I needed to include some little stories, anecdotes about the things that had happened there. "Oh my God, is that man crazy?" I thought. How many—if any— stories could be found in a parking lot where some kids play? As it turned out, a lot.

With each draft came more stories and more characters. Twelve drafts later, after countless sessions with my editor, we finally finished it. This was the first time that I actually noticed how much the finished product differed, for the better, from the first draft. Revisions are to be expected, and they help make the work better. When I write now, I go over a paragraph—and sometimes a sentence—ten or twenty times, trying to get it to sound right. All this before I even show it to anyone.

Are there any important things you've learned about the writing process?

TROY SEAN: You should allow yourself to talk to the computer or paper as you would a friend. This gives your piece a voice—your voice. If a friend reads your work, she should be able to say: "I know who wrote this; this sounds like something my friend would say."

One way to give a piece a voice is by using expressions that you usually use. If you know that you would normally say, "I thought that was wild," don't write something like, "I found it to be extremely entertaining."

I used to waste a lot of time trying to find the best way to say things, looking for the biggest and most intelligent-sounding words to express my thoughts. It wasn't until I became the editor of a school publication that I realized that searching for big words not only wastes time, it doesn't even improve the writing. I had one writer who always used these elaborate words. When reading his pieces, I'd focus more on the big words than the general message. Most readers don't want to have to pull out a thesaurus in order to understand what the writer is saying. Those big, intelligent-sounding words can make a reader lose interest in the story. So when you write, do it as though you're speaking to another person and you'll become a better writer.

ANITA: I've learned to question myself a lot more and to explore transient ideas further than I would have before. By the time the final draft is done, I've learned a lot more about myself. I usually find that I have a lot of ideas and feelings about the subject that I had not explored before.

MOHAMAD: The personal essay goes beyond the facts, figures, and analysis of "news" reporting. It helps us put information into context, so we can interpret our lives and explore our emotions.

THE REWARDS OF WRITING

So given all the effort involved, why do you keep writing? What do you get out of it? What do you like about it?

LORETTA: My friends and family know that I've written a few articles and assume that writing is something I love to do. That is true but it is also false. I don't love to write. What I love is to see the results of my writing—that is, if it has turned out well. There is great satisfaction in completing something that is well-written and thought-provoking.

ZEENA: After "Home Is Where the Hurt Is" was published, I got numerous letters from the people who read it. It was amazing how people all over New York City were reacting to what I had written—and they didn't even know my name. I remember one letter in particular from an adult who was also South Asian and had been in a similar situation. She was pleased that I wrote the story, adding in a little note at the end that "it would have helped a lot" if she had read something like this when she was a teen. It brought tears to my eyes! All of a sudden, I felt a bond with a stranger (the miracle of writing!). Most of all, those letters convinced me that I had been right—I could help others through writing about myself.

FERENTZ: I've realized that although it's my name on the byline, my friends and I are all in the story, and the more people who read it, the better. Because more people will care—not only about me but about my friends and all the other guys like us who are out there.

Now I'm more at ease with putting my feelings on paper, and even look forward to it, because I'm a writer and that's what writers do. I've learned that having the ability to write is a gift because by using words you get to illustrate things that others only dream about.

The essays in this anthology originally appeared in the following editions of New Youth Connections.

"Brotherly Love" by Jessica Vicuña, March 1996

"How to Survive Shopping with Mom" by Chris Kanarick, March 1992

"A Shortcut to Independence" by Anita Chikkatur, September/October 1994

"My Father: I Want to Be Everything He's Not" by Troy Sean Welcome, May/June 1994

"Dad's Home Cooking" by Loretta Chan, May/June 1995

"Saying Goodbye to Uncle Nick" by Josbeth Lebron, April 1995

"Home Is Where the Hurt Is" by Zeena Bhattacharya, September/October and November 1993

"The Crew from the Parking Lot" by Ferentz Lafargue, November 1992

"At Home in Coney Island" by Sheila Maldonado, September/October 1991

"Antigua: Almost Paradise" by Jillian Braithwaite, December 1991

"Chinese in New York, American in Beijing" by Kim Hoang, May/June 1995

"A 'Nice' Neighborhood...Where Nobody Knows My Name" by Sung Park, May/June 1995

"Revenge in the Hood: A Deadly Game" by Michelle Rodney, January/February 1995

"I Ain't Got No Culture" by Lara Coopéy, December, 1992

"Yo, Hollywood! Where Are the Latinos At?" by Jessica Vicuña, May/June 1994

"Color Me Different" by Jamal Greene, September/October 1994

"The 'N' Word: It Just Slips Out" by Allen Francis, January/February 1994

"My Lebanese Passport" by Mohamad Bazzi, January/February 1993

"Asian by Association" by Jessica Vicuña, May/June 1995

"My Journey Home" by Anna Song, November 1987

"Single and Lovin' It" by Latrice Davis, December 1993

"Dream Girl" by Rance Scully, September/October 1995

"Tired of Being a Target" by Loretta Chan, September/October 1993

"A Girl Takes Control" by Troy Sean Welcome, April 1994

"I Hated Myself" by David Miranda, April, May, and June 1993

"What Would You Do If I Was Gay?" by Gina Trapani, December 1992

"My First Love: Too Much, Too Soon" by Anonymous, April and May/June 1994

"Becoming a Vegetarian: A Matter of Taste" by Victoria Law, January/February 1995

"A Designer Addiction" by Delia Cleveland, April 1994

"A Rap Fan's Alternative" by Allen Francis, November 1994

"Moving into the Mainstream" by Slade Anderson, June 1993

"Climbing the Golden Arches" by Marissa Nuñez, June 1993

"Growing into Fatherhood" by Julio Pagan, May 1992

"My Road Doesn't Lead to College" by Brandy Scelzo, January/February 1995

"Dorm Life Is Heaven" by Donna Hutchinson, December 1995

SUBJECT GUIDE TO ESSAYS

Index to Essays by Form

TRAVELOGUE

ACKNOWLEDGMENTS

New Youth Connections, the magazine in which these essays first appeared, would not exist without the support of adults who strongly believe in freedom of expression for young people, even when their writing explores issues that many people would prefer to keep under wraps. Four adults inspired the creation of *New Youth Connections* and gave generously of their time and advice long before we had published a single issue: David Hackett, John B. Simon, Sister Ann Heintz, and Craig Trygstad.

David Hackett, Executive Director of the Robert F. Kennedy Memorial, gave us our first financial support. John Simon, Executive Director of the DOME Project, a New York City youth program, recruited our first teen staff and provided free office space and emergency loans which kept us afloat in our earliest days. Sister Ann Heintz and her colleague Craig Trygstad founded *New Expression*, the magazine on which we modeled *New Youth Connections*.

NYC has flourished for nearly two decades because of the support of thousands of other adults—far too many to list here. Teachers, counselors, administrators, and librarians have used the magazine to convey information, prompt discussion, and teach writing. Youth program staff and young adult librarians have loyally circulated the magazine to teens for many years.

New Youth Connections is published by Youth Communication, a nonprofit corporation which is dependent on foundation and corporation grants for over eighty percent of its support. Major contributors to *New Youth Connections* and Youth Communication include AT&T, the Vincent Astor Foundation, the Bay Foundation, the Booth Ferris Foundation, the Catalog for Giving, the Aaron Diamond Foundation, Chase Manhattan Bank, the Child Welfare Fund, Citibank, the Edna McConnell Clark Foundation, the Cummings Memorial Fund, the William T. Grant Foundation, the Charles Hayden Foundation, the Edward W. Hazen Foundation, the Esther & Joseph Klingenstein Foundation, the Hearst Foundation, the Heckscher Foundation for Children, the Edward S. Moore Foundation, JP Morgan, the Morgan Stanley Foundation, The New York Community Trust, the New York Foundation, The New York Times Co. Foundation, Newsday, the Paul Rapoport Foundation, the Scherman Foundation, Seagrams, the Tides Foundation, Time Warner, the WKBJ Partnership Foundation, the DeWitt Wallace-Reader's Digest Fund Inc., the Albert & Bessie Warner Fund, and several anonymous donors. We are deeply grateful for their support.

NYC depends upon collaboration and contributions of the entire Youth Communication staff. Tom Brown, who has written "Tips for Teachers," a newsletter that accompanies each issue of *NYC*, oversees the magazine's distribution and plays a key role in keeping *NYC* financially secure through fundraising and subscription management. Efrain Reyes is responsible for the desktop publishing and design of each issue and for maintaining a cantankerous batch of computers in the *NYC* newsroom. Omar Lewis, Pek Lan Wong, Sal Serna and Tony Savino have trained the teen artists and photographers who make *NYC* exciting to look at. Since 1990, Jim Fishel has volunteered as our advertising sales director, bringing in much needed revenue.

We would especially like to acknowledge former *NYC* editors Al Desetta, Carol Kelly, Duffie Cohen, and Vivian Louie, who worked with some of the writers whose stories appear in this book and made important contributions to the magazine's growth, as did the other editors who have worked at *NYC* over the years: Tony McGinty, Donna Lawson, Alyson Reid, Lynda Hill, Lisa Abramson, Sean Chambers, Louis Young, Richard Irizarry, and Kimberly Smith.

While some *NYC* writers find us on their own, many others are referred to us by teachers, counselors, and other youth workers. We are grateful to the New York City Board of Education's Executive Internship program and the City-As-School alternative high schools for making it possible for dozens of high school students (including almost half of the writers included in this anthology) to get academic credit for their work here.

Youth Communication is governed by a Board of Directors, two of whom, William Josephson and Sandra Silverman, have served the program from its earliest days. All Board members have donated generously of their time and talent and made important contributions to our success.

Diana Autin taught us how to write our first foundation proposals, and has contributed advice and support in countless ways ever since.

In addition, Andrea Estepa wishes to thank her parents for their constant love and support, which makes everything easier; her friends Darrel Schoeling and Joan Jubela for reading and commenting on the introduction; and contributors Zeena Bhattacharya, Ferentz Lafargue, Mohamad Bazzi, Loretta Chan, Troy Sean Welcome and Anita Chikkatur for devoting so much time and energy to explaining why and how they write and for remaining patient and good-humored through so many revisions.

Keith Hefner
Andrea Estepa
Philip Kay

About Youth Communication

𝒴outh Communication is a nonprofit youth development program located in New York City, whose mission is to teach writing, journalism, and leadership skills. The teenagers we train, most of whom are New York City public high school students, become writers for our two teen-written publications, *New Youth Connections*, a general interest youth magazine, and *Foster Care Youth United*, a magazine for young people in foster care.

Youth Communication was founded in 1980 by Keith Hefner in response to a nationwide study which found that the high school press was characterized by censorship, mediocrity and racial exclusion. Hefner has won a Charles H. Revson Fellowship at Columbia University and the Luther P. Jackson Excellence in Education Award from the New York Association of Black Journalists for his work at Youth Communication, and in 1989 he won a MacArthur "genius" Fellowship.

Each year, more than one hundred young people participate in Youth Communication's school-year and summer journalism workshops. They come from every corner of New York City, and the vast majority are African American, Latino, or Asian. The teen staff members work under the direction of several full-time adult editors in our Manhattan offices, which are equipped with two newsrooms, a score of computers, two darkrooms, an art department, and a desktop publishing and production department.

Teachers, counselors, social workers, and other adults circulate our magazines to young people in their classes and after-school youth programs. They distribute 70,000 copies of *New Youth Connections* each month during the school year, and 10,000 bimonthly copies of *Foster Care Youth United*. Teachers frequently tell us that teens in their classes—including students who are ordinarily resistant to reading—clamor for these publications. For our teen writers, the opportunity to reach their peers with important self-help information, and with accurate portrayals of their lives, motivates them to create powerful stories.

Running a strong youth development program, while simultaneously producing quality teen magazines requires a balance between a process that is sensitive to the complicated lives and emotions of the teen participants, and one that is intellectually rigorous. We sustain that balance in the writing/teaching/editing relationship, which is the core of our program.

Our teaching and editorial process begins with discussions between adult editors and the teen staff, during which they seek to discover the stories that are most important to each teen writer and that will also appeal to a significant segment of our reading public.

Once topics have been chosen, students begin the process of crafting their stories. For a personal story, that means revisiting events in one's past to understand their significance for the future. For a commentary, it means developing a logical and persuasive argument. For a reported story, it means gathering information through research and interviews. Students look inward and outward as they try to make sense of their experiences and the world around them, and find the points of intersection between personal and social concerns. That process can take a few weeks, or a few months. Stories frequently go through four, five, or more drafts as students work on them under the guidance of editors in the same way that any professional writer does.

Many of the students who walk through our doors have uneven

skills, as a result of poor education, living under extremely stressful conditions, or coming from homes where English is a second language. Yet, to complete their stories, students must successfully perform a wide range of activities, including writing and rewriting, reading, discussion, reflection, research, interviewing, and typing. They must work as members of a team, and they must accept a great deal of individual responsibility. They learn to read subway maps, verify facts, and cope with rejection. They engage in explorations of truthfulness and fairness. They meet deadlines. They must develop the audacity to believe that they have something important to say, and the humility to recognize that saying it well is not a process of instant gratification, but usually requires a long, hard struggle through many discussions and much rewriting.

It would be impossible to teach these skills and dispositions as separate, disconnected topics, like grammar, ethics, or assertiveness training. However, we find that students make rapid progress when they are learning skills in the context of an inquiry that is personally significant to them, and which they think will benefit their peers.

Writers usually participate in our program for one semester, though some stay much longer. Years later, many of them report that working here was a turning point in their lives—that it helped them acquire the confidence and skills that they needed for success in their subsequent education and careers. Scores of our graduates have overcome tremendous obstacles to become journalists, writers, and novelists. Hundreds more are working in law, teaching, business, and other careers.

New Youth Connections, where all of the essays in this anthology were originally published, was founded to give a voice to the young people of New York City. Conceived and planned by Keith Hefner and founding editor Tony McGinty, the magazine began publication in May, 1980. It is circulated in over four hundred New York City public high schools, libraries, and youth programs.

Over the years teachers have assigned many thousands of in-class essays based on stories in the magazine. Teen readers say that the information and inspiration that *NYC* provides helps them reflect on their lives and opens lines of communication with parents and teachers.

Many of *NYC*'s teen staff members have made a career of writing, including National Book Award finalist Edwidge Danticat (*Krik? Krak!*), novelist James Hardy (*B-Boy Blues*), memoirist and editor Veronica Chambers (*Mama's Girl*) and *New York Times* reporter Rachel Swarns.

ABOUT THE EDITORS

*A*NDREA ESTEPA has been an editor of *New Youth Connections*, a magazine written by and for New York City young people, since 1991. Prior to that she was a reporter for the *Hartford Courant* and the *Los Angeles Times*. She has a Master's Degree from the Columbia University School of Journalism and a Bachelor's Degree from Brown University.

PHILIP KAY has been an editor of *New Youth Connections* since 1990. He also teaches journalism at the City University of New York's Hunter College. He has a Master's Degree in Spanish, as well as a Bachelor's Degree, from New York University.

Both Estepa and Kay have been awarded Charles H. Revson Fellowships on the Future of The City of New York at Columbia University.

They are also the editors, with Al Desetta, of two other books by Youth Communication, *Out With It: Gay and Straight Teens Write About Homosexuality* (1996) and *Things Get Hectic: Urban Teens Write About the Violence that Surrounds Them* (1998).

CPSIA information can be obtained
at www.ICGtesting.com
Printed in the USA
BVHW031300300821
615610BV00001B/1

9 780892 553761